Retreat Ideas

for Ministry with Young Teens

Heads-up | Easy | Low-Cost | Purposeful

Retreat Ideas

for Ministry with Young Teens

edited by Marilyn Kielbasa

Heads-up | Easy | Low-Cost | Purposeful

Saint Mary's Press
Christian Brothers Publications
Winona, Minnesota

Genuine recycled paper with 10% post-consumer waste.
Printed with soy-based ink.

The publishing team included Marilyn Kielbasa, development editor; Rebecca Fairbank, copy editor; Barbara Bartelson, production editor; Hollace Storkel, typesetter; Cindi Ramm, art director; Kenneth Hey, cover and logo designer; cover images, PhotoDisc Inc.; produced by the graphics division of Saint Mary's Press.

The development consultants for the HELP (Heads-up, Easy, Low-Cost, and Purposeful) series included the following people:

Sarah Bush, Pewee Valley, Kentucky

Jeanne Fairbanks, Tipp City, Ohio

Carole Goodwin, Louisville, Kentucky

Joe Grant, Louisville, Kentucky

Maryann Hakowski, Yorktown, Virginia

Jo Joy, Temple, Texas

Kevin Kozlowski, New Carlisle, Ohio

Jennifer MacArthur, Saint Louis, Missouri

David Nissen, Cincinnati, Ohio

Ruthie Nonnenkamp, Prospect, Kentucky

The retreats in this book were created by the following contributors:

Lisa-Marie Calderone-Stewart

Carole Goodwin

Joe Grant

Maryann Hakowski

Ruthie Nonnenkamp

The acknowledgments continue on page 140.

Printed in the United States of America

Printing: 9 8 7 6 5 4 3 2 1

Year: 2009 08 07 06 05 04 03 02 01

ISBN 0-88489-540-8

Library of Congress Cataloging-in-Publication Data

Kielbasa, Marilyn.
    Retreat ideas for ministry with young teens / Marilyn Kielbasa.
    p. cm.—(HELP)
ISBN 0-88489-540-8 (pbk.)
    1. Retreats for youth. 2. Church work with teenagers. I. Title. II. HELP (Series : Winona, Minn.)
BV4447 .K53 2001
269'.23—dc21
                                                                                    2001000837

Contents

Introduction

Retreat Ideas for Ministry with Young Teens is one of seven books in the HELP series—a collection of **H**eads-up, **E**asy, **L**ow-Cost, and **P**urposeful activities for young adolescents. These strategies are designed to be used as part of a comprehensive youth ministry program for grades six to eight. The strategies can stand alone or complement a religious education curriculum.

The other books in the HELP series are as follows:

⊚ *Community-Building Ideas for Ministry with Young Teens*
⊚ *Family Ideas for Ministry with Young Teens*
⊚ *Hands-on Ideas for Ministry with Young Teens*
⊚ *Holiday and Seasonal Ideas for Ministry with Young Teens*
⊚ *Justice and Service Ideas for Ministry with Young Teens*
⊚ *Prayer Ideas for Ministry with Young Teens*

These books are helpful resources for anyone who works with young adolescents in a church or school setting. They can provide a strong foundation for a year-round, total youth ministry program whose goal is to evangelize young adolescents and support them in their faith journey.

Overview of This Book

Retreat Ideas for Ministry with Young Teens may be used by a coordinator of youth ministry, a director of religious education, catechists, teachers, a parish youth ministry team, or any adult who works with young teens. Ownership of the book includes permission to duplicate any part of it for use with program participants.

The book includes two overnight retreats and four one-day retreats. The themes of the overnight retreats are self-esteem and being true to oneself. The themes of the other four retreats are Confirmation, discipleship, the Triduum, and leadership development.

Format of the Retreats

Each retreat outline in this book begins with a brief description of its purpose. The next element is a suggested time for the activity. This is flexible and takes into account several variables, such as the size of the group, the number and length of breaks, and the comfort level of the participants. Use the suggested time as a starting point and modify it according to your circumstances.

Next is a description of the size of the group that the retreat was written for. Most of the retreats work with a range of group sizes. If your group is large, be sure to recruit enough adults to help with logistics and supervision. A good rule to follow is that for every six to eight young teens, one adult should be present. The leaders should be trained in the process of the retreat and in the dynamics of small-group leadership.

In some retreats a section on special considerations follows the one on group size. It includes things such as notices about remote preparation requirements and cautions to pay special attention to a particular developmental issue of early adolescence.

A complete checklist of materials needed is the next part of the presentation of every retreat. A detailed description of the retreat's procedure is then provided, followed by alternative approaches. Those alternatives may be helpful in adapting the retreat to the needs of your group and your schedule.

The final element in each retreat offers space for keeping notes about how you might want to use the retreat in the future or change it to fit the needs of your group.

Programming Ideas

The retreats in this book can be used in a variety of ways. Consider the following suggestions:

- The program coordinator, catechists, teachers, and coordinator of youth ministry may collaborate to plan a retreat as part of the religious education program.
- Plan a daylong retreat during the summer months, when most young adolescents are less busy and may be open to a variety of activities. Youth ministers may use such retreats as part of a strong summer program for young teens.
- Schoolteachers may schedule a day of reflection to supplement their day-to-day curriculum.

Standard Materials

Many of the items in the materials checklists are common to several retreats and other strategies in the series. To save time consider gathering frequently used materials in convenient bins and storing those bins in a place that is accessible to all staff and volunteer leaders. Some recommendations for how to organize such bins follow.

Supply Bin
The following items frequently appear in materials checklists:
- Bibles, at least one for every two participants
- masking tape
- cellophane tape
- washable and permanent markers (thick and thin)
- pens or pencils
- self-stick notes
- scissors
- newsprint
- blank paper, scrap paper, and notebook paper
- postcards
- notepaper
- envelopes
- baskets
- candles and matches
- items to create a prayer space (e.g., a colored cloth, a cross, a bowl of water, and a vase for flowers)

Craft Bin
Many of the retreats use craft activities to involve the young people. Consider collecting the following supplies in a separate bin:
- construction paper
- yarn and string, in assorted colors
- poster board
- glue and glue sticks
- fabric paints
- glitter and confetti
- used greeting cards
- beads
- modeling clay
- paintbrushes and paints
- crayons
- used magazines and newspapers
- hole punches

- scissors
- stickers of various kinds
- index cards
- gift wrap and ribbon

Music Bin

Young people often find deep and profound meaning in the music and lyrics of songs, both past and present. Also, the right music can set an appropriate mood for a prayer or activity. Begin with a small collection of tapes or CDs in a music bin and add to it over time. You might ask the young people to put some of their favorite music in the bin. The bin might include the following styles of music:

- *Fun gathering music that is neither current nor popular with young teens.* Ideas are well-known classics (e.g., *Overture to William Tell, Stars and Stripes Forever,* and *1812 Overture*), songs from musical theater productions, children's songs, and Christmas songs for use any time of the year.
- *Prayerful, reflective instrumental music, such as the kind that is available in the adult alternative, or New Age, section of music stores.* Labels that specialize in this type of music include Windham Hill and Narada.
- *Popular songs with powerful messages.* If you are not well versed in popular music, ask the young people to offer suggestions.
- *The music of contemporary Christian artists.* Most young teens are familiar with Amy Grant, Michael W. Smith, and Steven Curtis Chapman. Also include the work of Catholic musicians, such as David W. Kauffman, Steve Angrisano, Bruce Deaton, Sarah Hart, Jesse Manibusan, and Jessica Alles.

Other Helpful Resources

In addition to the seven books in the HELP series, the following resources can be useful in your ministry with young adolescents. All the books in the following list are published by Saint Mary's Press and can be obtained by calling or writing us at the phone number and address listed in the "Your Comments or Suggestions" section at the end of this introduction.

Catechism Connection for Teens series, by Lisa Calderone-Stewart and Ed Kunzman (1999).
   That First Kiss and Other Stories
   My Wish List and Other Stories
   Better Than Natural and Other Stories
   Straight from the Heart and Other Stories
   Meeting Frankenstein and Other Stories
   The five books in this collection contain short, engaging stories for teens on the joys and struggles of adolescent life, each story with a reflection con-

necting it to a Catholic Christian belief. Each book's faith connections reflect teachings from a different part of the *Catechism of the Catholic Church.*

The Catholic Youth Bible, edited by Brian Singer-Towns (2000). The most youth-friendly Bible for Catholic teens available. The scriptural text is accompanied by hundreds of articles to help young people pray, study, and live the Scriptures.

Faith Works for Junior High: Scripture- and Tradition-Based Sessions for Faith Formation, by Lisa-Marie Calderone-Stewart (1993). A series of twelve active meeting plans on various topics related to the Scriptures and church life.

Guided Meditations for Junior High: Good Judgment, Gifts, Obedience, Inner Blindness, by Jane E. Ayer (1997). Four guided meditations for young teens, available on audiocassette or compact disc. A leader's guide includes the script and programmatic options. Other volumes in this series, called A Quiet Place Apart, will also work with young teens.

Looking Past the Sky: Prayers by Young Teens, edited by Marilyn Kielbasa (1999). A collection of 274 prayers by and for young adolescents in grades six to eight.

One-Day Retreats for Junior High Youth, by Geri Braden-Whartenby and Joan Finn Connelly (1997). Six retreats that each fit into a school day or an afternoon or evening program. Each retreat contains a variety of icebreakers, prayers, group exercises, affirmations, and guided meditations.

Prayers with Pizzazz for Junior High Teens, by Judi Lanciotti (1996). A variety of creative prayer experiences that grab young teens' attention. The prayers are useful in many different settings, such as classes, meetings, prayer services, and retreats.

ScriptureWalk Junior High: Bible Themes, by Maryann Hakowski (1999). Eight 90-minute sessions to help bring youth and the Bible together. Each session applies biblical themes to the life issues that concern young teens.

Connections to the Discovering Program

The Discovering Program, published by Saint Mary's Press, is a religious education program for young people in grades six to eight. It consists of fourteen six-session minicourses. Each session is 1 hour long and based on the principles of active learning.

The strategies in the HELP series cover themes that are loosely connected to those explored in the Discovering Program, and can be used as part of a total youth ministry program in which the Discovering curriculum is the central catechetical component. However, no strategy in the series presumes that the participants have taken a particular course in the Discovering Program, or requires that they do so. The appendices at the end of this book list the connections between the HELP retreats and the Discovering courses.

Your Comments or Suggestions

Saint Mary's Press wants to know your reactions to the retreats and strategies in the HELP series. We are also interested in new youth ministry strategies and retreats for use with young teens. If you have a comment or suggestion, please write the series editor, Marilyn Kielbasa, at 702 Terrace Heights, Winona, MN 55987-1320; call the editor at our toll-free number, 800-533-8095; or e-mail the editor at *mkielbasa@smp.org.* Your ideas will help improve future editions of these books.

Let Your Light Shine

An Overnight Retreat on Self-Esteem

OVERVIEW This overnight retreat on self-esteem invites the young people to explore their own personal gifts and encourages them to share those abilities with others. The retreat emphasizes the light of Christ in our life, the special people who bring us closer to Christ, and the ways we can be the light of Christ for others.

Suggested Time

This retreat covers about 13 hours, including recreation and nutrition breaks. It runs for about 4½ hours on the first day, beginning in the evening. The remainder of the retreat takes place on the second day, ending in the late afternoon. If your schedule is different, you may need to adapt the retreat to fit that schedule and maintain the proper flow.

Group Size

This retreat is most effective with groups of twenty or fewer. However, it can be done with any number of young people, divided into small groups, each led by an older teen or adult.

Special Preparations

Well before the retreat, contact the parents of the participants. Ask them to write a letter of love and affirmation to their child, telling their child why and how he or she is the light of Christ for the family. Stress that the letter should be more than just a short note and should truly come from the heart. The teens should not know about the letters until they receive them on the retreat.

Provide clear delivery instructions. Emphasize that every participant must have a letter from a parent. The activity will have to be canceled if even one letter is missing.

Materials Needed

- colored construction paper
- double-stick tape, straight pins, or safety pins
- a large pillar candle and matches
- 3-by-5-inch index cards, two for each person
- inexpensive notebooks, one for each person
- used magazines
- scissors, one for each person
- glue sticks, at least one for every three people
- pens or pencils
- colored markers
- masking tape
- copies of handout 1, "Let Your Light Shine," one for each person
- a tape or CD player, and a recording of reflective music (optional)
- empty baby food jars, one for each person
- a variety of brightly colored tissue paper
- household white glue
- paper plates, one for each person
- clear shellac or decoupage covering, such as Mod Podge
- paintbrushes, no larger than one inch, one for every two or three people
- votive candles, one for each person
- one or more strings of Christmas lights with screw-in bulbs
- a basket or box
- a Bible
- one copy of resource 1, "Christmas Island: A Parable of Light"
- copies of handout 2, "The Lord Is My Light and My Salvation," one for each person
- parish songbooks, one for each person (optional)
- newsprint
- small prizes (optional)
- balloons, one for each person

- ☀ small pieces of paper, about 3-by-3-inches, one for each person
- ☀ permanent markers
- ☀ letters from parents
- ☀ blindfolds, one for each person
- ☀ copies of handout 3, "Dimming the Light of Christ," one for each person
- ☀ a flashlight (optional)
- ☀ a large solid-colored bowl (optional)
- ☀ poster board, one sheet for each small group
- ☀ rulers, one for each small group
- ☀ plain paper or notebook paper
- ☀ envelopes, one for each person
- ☀ a wick or taper candle

PROCEDURE

Part 1: Getting Started (90 to 110 minutes)

Welcome, Introductions, and Prayer

Preparation. Using as many different colors of construction paper as you want small groups, cut out name tags in the shape of bulbs from a string of holiday lights, like this:

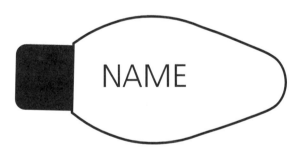

You will need as many bulbs as young people on the retreat. Cut an equal number of bulbs from each color of paper so that the small groups will be roughly equal in size. Write one participant's name on each bulb.

Set up tables (preferably round ones) and chairs. Have as many chairs around each table as you want people in a small group.

Set up a prayer space in front of the group with a large pillar candle.

1. As the participants arrive, give each of them a lightbulb-shaped name tag and a safety pin, double-stick tape, or a straight pin to attach the tag to their clothing.

2. Enthusiastically welcome the young teens to the retreat and introduce the team members. Since for some participants this is likely to be their first retreat, you may want to discuss the idea of a retreat with them by asking the following questions:

What is the purpose of a retreat?

What do you think will happen on this retreat?

What do you hope will happen?

What do you hope will *not* happen?

You might also go over some of the basic ground rules for the event and your expectations of them. Keep this presentation upbeat and positive to set the proper mood.

3. Introduce the theme of the retreat by making the following points in your own words:

The theme for this retreat is "Let Your Light Shine." The retreat focuses on the light of Christ in our life and how that light shines in our relationship with ourselves, others, and God.

The topics include these:

What do you have to share?

How do you let your light shine?

Who are the people who light your way to Christ?

Who are the people and things that put out the light of Christ?

How do you spread the light of Christ at home, in school, and with friends?

It is important that everyone participate for us to enjoy this retreat as a group and as individuals. Everyone's input is important.

Tell the young people to think about the Christmas lights that their family uses to decorate during the holiday season. Then ask them what happens when one bulb burns out. The answer is that with many brands of lights, all the lights go out when one burns out. Continue with your presentation, making the following points in your own words:

Imagine that we—as a group—are a string of lights. Our faith joins our string of lights together.

Jesus asks us to be a light for all people. Try not to let your light go out. Try not to put another person's light out. We need to encourage one another and challenge one another on this retreat and in our life.

4. Light the pillar candle in the prayer space. As you are doing so, make the point that the candle reminds us that Christ is the light of the world and that he is always with us. Note that the candle will burn through all the retreat activities to keep the light of Christ shining among us.

Say a spontaneous prayer asking God's blessings on the retreat, on the team, and on the young people, so that everyone will be able to see Jesus in themselves and in others. Invite the young people to pause and silently ask Jesus to answer any special prayers of petition they bring to this retreat. After a pause, end the prayer by saying the following:

We ask all these things in the name of Jesus Christ, our Lord and Savior, who is the light of our world. Amen.

Icebreaker: Let Your Light Shine

Preparation. Write each of the following words on six index cards. You will need one card for each young person. If you have more than forty-eight participants, add different kinds of lights. If you have fewer than forty-two, eliminate the appropriate number of lights. Mix up the cards before distributing them.

- candle
- flashlight
- lightbulb
- streetlight
- night-light
- refrigerator light
- laser light
- fluorescent light

1. Provide each young person with a chair. Ask the participants to arrange the chairs in a circle. Remove one chair from the circle and ask that person to stand in the middle.

Explain that the person in the middle can call out one type of light, two or more types of light, or say, "Let your light shine." Whoever is holding a card matching the light that was called out must get up and find a new chair, as must the person in the middle. Give the following examples:

If the person in the middle calls out, "lightbulb," everyone holding lightbulb cards must find another chair.

If "candles" and "flashlights" are called, everyone holding those cards must find a new chair.

If the person in the middle says, "Let your light shine," everyone must find a new chair.

The person left without a chair is the new person in the center.

No one is permitted to push another person out of a chair. If the teens play too rough, stop the game and ask them to take it easy before resuming play. Allow about 15 minutes for this activity.

Small-Group Formation: String of Lights

1. Ask the young people to find those who have the same color name tag as they do. Once the groups have assembled, direct them each to sit down at a table.

2. Allow a few minutes for each person to introduce himself or herself to the small group. You might ask the participants to share something in addition to their name, such as, the farthest place they have ever visited or their favorite toy when they were five years old.

Tell the young teens that they will be working in small groups for many of the activities and discussions during the retreat. The small groups offer a great place to share ideas, make new friends, and encourage one another to "let your light shine."

Part 2: Seeing the Light in Yourself (90 minutes)

Notebook Activity: Spotlight on You

1. Give each person a notebook. Place used magazines, scissors, glue sticks, pens or pencils, and other craft supplies on each table. Tell the teens that they are to search through the magazines for words and photographs that describe their abilities and positive qualities, and then cut these out and glue them onto the cover of their notebook. For example, if someone is a serious student and a good friend, she or he should find words and pictures that relate to those qualities. Remind the young people that this activity is not about likes and dislikes. Just because a person likes a particular music group does not mean that it belongs on the cover. A person's collage is about who she or he is as a person.

Allow 30 minutes for the young people to complete this part of the project.

2. Ask the young people to share with their small group why they chose some of the words and photographs. They should share at least five examples, but they are welcome to share everything on their cover if they choose to.

3. Tell the participants to put their name and the date of the retreat on the first page of their journal notebook. On the next page, ask them to write down five items from their collage that they want to try and remember. For example,

if someone put the word *super* on the cover, they may need to remember that they have a lot of good inside them. If someone pasted a heart on their journal, they may want to remember that the love they have needs to be shared with more people.

4. Close the activity by reminding the young people that sometimes we have to put ourselves in the spotlight and take a close look at all the good we have to share and how much we have to offer. Encourage everyone to "let their light shine" throughout the retreat and beyond.

Small-Group Activity: Shed Light on the Matter

Preparation. Identify Scripture passages that include the word *light* as part of the phrase. You will need as many phrases as you have small groups. Here are some examples:

◎ You are the light of the world. (Matt. 5:14)
◎ The Lord is my light and my salvation. (Ps. 27:1)
◎ Your light must shine before all people. (Matt. 5:16)
◎ You must live like people who belong in the light. (Eph. 5:8)
◎ The light of Christ has come into the world. (John 1:9)

Assign one phrase to each group, and divide the words in the phrase among members of each group. For example, if a group has six members, you might divide the phrase in the following way:

◎ The—Lord—is my—light—and my—salvation.

Use a different color of index card or a different color marker for each passage. On each card, write the person's name on one side and her or his assigned part of the Scripture passage on the other. Scramble all the cards and place them name-side up on a large table.

1. Announce that each person should find the card with his or her name on it. When the participants have found their card, they are to find the other people with cards of the same color or same color of ink in which their names are written. Then they are to unscramble the scriptural verse and stand in order, holding their word(s) in front of them.

2. When all the groups have figured out their scriptural verse, ask them to spend 5 minutes discussing what meaning the passage might hold for them.

After the discussion ask a spokesperson from each group to share some of its responses with the large group. When all the responses have been shared, direct the small groups to tape their scriptural verse together and post it in the meeting room.

Presentation and Reflection: We Are the Light of Christ

Preparation. If possible, recruit an older teenager to prepare and deliver the following witness talk.

1. The purpose of this presentation is to encourage the young people to recognize the light of Christ within themselves. Ask the teen volunteer to make the following points in her or his own words, expanding the points by sharing personal stories and feelings about her or his struggle for self-worth. Direct the presenter to offer strategies for building confidence in everyday life. (If no teen presenter is available, the leader will need to make this presentation.)

 God has given us all special gifts and talents. We are each unique and valuable. Each one of us has the light of Christ within us. We need to recognize that light within ourselves.

Think about the following questions:

What are some of your gifts and talents?

How has God made you different from others?

How do you feel about yourself?

Many people put themselves down all the time. For some reason it is often difficult to see the good in oneself. But it is important to feel good about oneself and to believe in oneself.

We also hurt the self-image of others by some of the things we say and do. Give concrete examples of how we can build up the self-image of others.

Jesus built up the self-esteem of others. For example, he ate with tax collectors, made time for little children, and washed the disciples' feet.

We also need to recognize the light of Christ in ourselves and in others and to do whatever we can to let it shine.

2. Distribute handout 1. Invite the participants to take their journal notebook and the handout questions to a place in the room where they can be alone with their thoughts. Encourage them to move away from other people so that they are not distracted. Allow about 10 minutes of quiet time for the teens to write their answers in their notebook. If you have reflective music available, begin playing it at this time.

3. After everyone is finished, call the participants back to their small groups. Encourage them to share their answers to the questions with their small group. However, assure them that they do not have to share everything. Allow about 10 minutes for small-group sharing.

If time permits, invite volunteers to share their answers to the last two questions with the large group. Close the activity by encouraging the young people to put into practice their ideas for building up themselves and one another.

Nutrition and Recreation Break

Part 3: We Hold the Light (50 to 60 minutes)

Candleholder Project

Preparation. Soak baby food jars in water to remove the labels. Make a sample candleholder, following the directions given in step 2 below.

During the break put the jars, scissors, tissue paper, glue, paper plates, shellac or Mod Podge, paintbrushes, and votive candles on each small-group table.

1. Introduce the activity by displaying the sample candleholder that you created before the retreat. Explain that the baby food jars represent each one of us. The candles represent Jesus and his light shining through each one of us.

2. Explain in your own words the following directions for making the candleholder:

Cut the tissue paper into ¹/₂-half-inch squares.

Glue the squares onto the baby food jars, overlapping the edges to create a stained-glass effect. Cover the bottom, sides, and top edges of the jar.

Wipe excess glue from the outside of the jar. Place the jar upside down on a paper plate and use a paintbrush to cover the jar with one coat of clear shellac or decoupage. (Note: Avoid placing jars on newspaper since the ink often adheres to the jar.)

When the jar is dry, place a votive candle inside.

As the young people are finishing their candleholder, set up for the prayer service in the prayer area.

Prayer Service: The People in Darkness Have Seen a Great Light

Preparation. Obtain one or more strings of Christmas lights with screw-in bulbs. Be sure to have one bulb available for each participant. Check the lights to make sure that all the bulbs work.

Remove all the bulbs from the sockets and place them in a box or basket. Arrange the cord of empty sockets on the floor in the shape of a cross. Leave it unplugged, but be sure you can access an outlet without disturbing the cross formation.

Place the unlit pillar candle and a Bible in the prayer space. Dim the lights in the room so that there is barely enough light to see.

Recruit a volunteer to read John 1:5–9. Practice reading the story in resource 1.

1. Gather the participants in the prayer space. Pass the basket or box of bulbs around the group and direct the teens to each take one.

2. When everyone has a bulb, call the group to a moment of silence in the presence of God. After a short pause, ask the volunteer to share the reading from John 1:5–9 and then light the pillar candle. Invite the teens to reflect silently on Jesus' great love for us.

3. After a few moments, read aloud the story from resource 1. Then ask the young people to think about the many people and other gifts from God that light up their lives. Invite them to take turns sharing a brief prayer of thanksgiving for those gifts. After doing so, have them screw their lightbulb into a socket near them.

4. When everyone has shared a prayer and screwed in a lightbulb, plug in the string(s) of lights. Allow a few seconds of silence so that the impact of the suddenly lit room registers with the teens. You may want to comment on the effect that being lights for one another can have in the world. Pray the following prayer or improvise one on the same theme:

Loving God, we thank you for giving us an abundance of gifts, including the people who love us. You also came to be with us in human form as Jesus, the light in our world.

Invite the teens to join hands as a symbol of unity, just as the string of lights is a symbol of the community of believers being light for one another. Lead them in praying the Lord's Prayer together.

5. Announce that the first part of the retreat is finished and that they will have a chance to explore further what it means to be a light for other people. Thank the young people for their participation and willingness to share their thoughts with others. Encourage them to leave the prayer area quietly and proceed to the sleeping areas. When the prayer space is empty, be sure to extinguish the candle and unplug the lights.

Part 4: The Lord Is My Light and My Salvation (120 minutes)

Morning Prayer

Preparation. Recruit two volunteers, one to read John 1:1–9 and the other, John 12:35–36.

Set up a prayer space with a Bible and the pillar candle that you used during the closing prayer in part 3.

If you have parish songbooks available, choose a song of praise that is familiar to the young people. You may want to practice the song before the prayer.

1. Gather the young people in the prayer space. Distribute handout 2 and copies of the parish songbook if they are available. Divide the group into two parts and designate one as group 1 and the other as group 2. Explain that when it is time to read the psalm, each group is to read its designated part, joining together for those sections that are preceded by the word *all*.

2. The order of the prayer follows:
◎ If you are using a song of praise, begin the prayer service by singing one verse of it together.
◎ Ask the first volunteer to read John 1:1–9.
◎ Pause for a few moments of silent reflection.
◎ Lead the young people in reciting Psalm 27 from handout 2.
◎ Light the pillar candle and invite the young people to offer prayers of petition, aloud or silently.
◎ Ask the second volunteer to read John 12:35–36.
◎ Lead the group in reciting the Lord's Prayer and the closing prayer on handout 2.
◎ If you used a song of praise to open the prayer, sing another verse to close it.

Focusing Exercise: Light and Sun Search

1. Ask the participants to gather with the small group that they were part of on the previous day. Give each small group a sheet of newsprint and some markers. Tell them to list all the songs they can think of that include the words *light* or *sun* in the lyrics. The songs can be contemporary, oldies, folk songs, children's songs, or whatever else they can think of. The participants should be able to recite the line that includes the word.

Allow about 3 minutes for the groups to complete the task, then compare results. Count only the songs for which someone in the group can recite the lyrics. If you have prizes available, award them to the group that came up with the longest list.

2. Close the exercise by sharing your observations. Include the following points:

The light of Christ is not always easy to find. We need to search for that light inside ourselves and in our world. Sometimes it is hard to remember the places and times when we have seen the light.

It is important to work together to find the light of Christ and to share it with one another. When one person shares his or her light, other people will recognize it and may share their own light.

Discussion and Presentation: Spotlight on Heroes

Preparation. Write the following questions on newsprint:
◎ Why would someone look up to the person on your balloon?
◎ From what you know about this person, what positive contribution does he or she make to the world?
◎ In what ways is this person a negative influence on popular culture?

Recruit someone, preferably an older teen or young adult, to give a 5- to 7-minute presentation on what it means to be a hero. Give that person adequate time to prepare her or his talk, based on the points in step 5.

1. Give each person a balloon, a small piece of paper, and a pen or pencil. Invite the young people to a moment of silence, and ask them to think of some-one in their life whom they consider to be a real hero. These are people whom they look up to and who light the way to Christ for them. Direct them to write the name of the person on the piece of paper.

When everyone has written a name, tell the teens to roll the paper tightly and put it in the balloon. They should then blow up the balloon and tie it off.

2. Make permanent markers available to the participants. Tell them to write on the outside of their balloon in large letters the name of a person whom popular culture holds up as a hero. You might need to give some suggestions, such as celebrities in the fields of athletics, movies, television, or music. Give the young people a minute or so to write a name on their balloon.

3. Explain that they all are to simultaneously throw their balloon in the air and shout the name of the person that is printed on the outside. The task of the group is to keep all the balloons from hitting the ground. Each time they hit a balloon, they are to shout the name written on it.

After 2 minutes or so, stop the activity and tell the young people to pick up any balloon that is near them and sit with their small group. The balloon they choose does not have to be their own.

4. Display the questions you wrote on newsprint before the retreat. Explain that the participants are to share with their group the name written on the balloon that they claimed and answer the questions listed on the newsprint with respect to that person. Note that all members of the small group can contribute their ideas about each celebrity.

5. Gather the young people in a circle and ask them to put their balloon aside. Invite the person that you recruited before the session to give his or her presentation on what it really means to be a hero. The talk should focus primarily on the ways other people help light our way to Christ and support and encourage us along the way. Advise the presenter to tell his or her personal story. The presenter might want to bring in pictures, posters, or other props.

Listed below are some questions and topics to consider in developing the talk.

Who are some of the cultural heroes you admire? Who did you admire when you were the age of the young teens in the group? Why do you or did you look up to these people?

What makes a true hero? What does being a hero have to do with being a light for others? Who are some of these heroes in your life? How do they light your way to Christ? How do you let these people know that they are your heroes?

How does Jesus light the way to the creator God? What are some ways that Jesus was a hero to others?

Close the talk by referring to the first reading during the morning prayer, taken from the Gospel of John, about the Word being made flesh. Emphasize the comparison between the word of God and a light shining in the darkness.

6. Direct the young people to reclaim the anonymous balloon that they had during the small-group discussion. Tell them to pop the balloon and take out the paper that is rolled up inside.

When everyone has popped their balloon and settled down, announce that you will pass the basket around the group. They are to share with the group the name on the paper by saying, "[Name] is a true hero." Then they are to put the paper in the basket and pass it along to the next person.

When the basket gets back to you, hold it up in offering. Say a spontaneous prayer thanking God for the true heroes in our life, that is, the people who light the way to God and encourage and support us along the way.

Place the basket near the candle and Bible in the prayer space, and encourage the young people to let their heroes know at some point what an effect they have.

Reflection: Letters from Parents

Preparation. Contact the parents of the young people about writing a letter of love and affirmation for their child. Collect the letters well before the retreat, taking care not to let the teens know about them.

If you do not have a letter from a parent for every participant, you may want to skip this section. Instead, give the letters to the participants at the end of the retreat to take home and read.

1. Explain that everyone will have a chance for some quiet time. Talk about the importance of being alone with one's thoughts periodically so that we have a chance to think about life and listen for God's voice.

Introduce the letters by making the following comments in your own words:

 Throughout the retreat we have been talking about how other people are the light in our life. We often fail to realize that we, too, can be the light for others. Some special people at home are thinking about you and praying for you right now. They are the light in your life, but you are light for them, too.

2. Distribute the letters and ask the young people to go to a place where they can be alone. Emphasize that the letters are to remain private. When they finish reading their letter, they are to put it away for safekeeping.

3. Close the activity by saying a short, spontaneous prayer thanking God for the people who love us. Encourage the teens to take their letter home, keep it in a safe place, and read it again and again, especially the next time they have a conflict with their parents or simply when they are feeling down.

Recreation and Nutrition Break

Part 5: Dimming the Light of Christ (60 to 75 minutes)

Presentation: Dimming Christ's Light

Preparation. Recruit someone to give a 5- to 7-minute talk about the things and people that dim the light of Christ in our life and what we can do to make the light of Christ shine brightly again. Give him or her the outline of talking points below.

If it is possible to do so, prepare the room by dimming the lights and closing the curtains or blinds.

1. Gather the young teens in the meeting space. Tell them that they will need their journal notebook. As they enter, give each one a blindfold. Explain that they are to find a comfortable place to sit. When they do, assist them with putting on their blindfold.

2. Ask the teens to name times when darkness is good. They might mention movie theaters, a bedroom when someone is trying to sleep, or outside when someone is looking at the stars.

Introduce the presentation with a comment that some people and things in our life dim the light of Christ. Invite the presenter to share his or her thoughts on the topic and include the following points:

Darkness is part of life. It always has been. Each day has a night. Even on sunny days, shadows are cast. Human beings generally do not like the darkness. We have lights, candles, flashlights, and many other ways to light up our world so that we don't have to stay in the dark. We believe that we have control over the light. If a room is dark, we simply turn on the light.

The light of Christ shines in our life, but sometimes his light grows dim. This dimming can be caused by people or things. For example, when someone puts us down or deliberately gets us in trouble, the light of Christ is dimmed. When we are obsessed with acquiring more and more things, when we put possessions before people, when making money becomes more important than God, the light of Christ is dimmed.

We sometimes dim the light of Christ by hurting others, by hurting ourselves, or by forgetting God in our life. Sin is a broken part of our relationship with God. It dims or even extinguishes the light of Christ that shines through us.

Some things we can do to rekindle that light include apologizing to and forgiving others, learning how to say no, and compromising. We can start believing in ourselves and using our gifts and talents the way God intended. We can pray more often and learn more about the Catholic faith.

The sacrament of Reconciliation, or Penance, plays an important role in restoring the light in our relationships with ourself, others, and God.

3. Allow a few moments of silence after the speaker is finished. Thank the presenter, then ask the young people what it was like to be blindfolded while the speaker was presenting. After they share their ideas, ask them to take off their blindfold.

Reflection and Discussion: Dimming the Light of Christ

1. Distribute copies of handout 3, and pens or pencils. Ask the young people to spend a few minutes answering the handout questions in their journal notebook. Allow at least 7 minutes for writing, though some young people may require or benefit from more time.

2. Gather the young people in their small groups and ask them to share their answers to the questions. Assure them that they do not have to share their answers to personal questions.

Recreation and Nutrition Break

Part 6: We Light the Way for Others (120 minutes)

Presentation: Sharing the Light of Christ

Preparation. Recruit someone to give a 5- to 7-minute talk about sharing the light by using one's gifts in the service of God and other people. Use Matt. 5:14–16 as a basis for the talk. The speaker may want to use a flashlight and a large solid-colored bowl to illustrate the scriptural passage. Give him or her the outline of talking points below, but encourage the speaker to use as many personal stories as time allows.

1. Gather the young people. Introduce the speaker and announce that he or she will be sharing what it means to be a light for others. The presenter should add personal stories and thoughts to make the following points:

Once we have received the light of Christ, we cannot keep it to ourselves. We must share it with others. [Give concrete examples of sharing the light at home, in school, and with friends.]

It is sometimes hard to keep the light from going out, particularly when we are up against peer pressure. Think about what Jesus gave the disciples that then gave them the courage to spread his light. The Holy Spirit helps us to share the light of Christ and to do his work on earth.

[Give examples of how one can share the light in the parish, family, and community. Identify people in the community—particularly young people— who make a difference.]

Sharing the light of Christ is a commitment. It is not a service project. It is not an occasional occurrence. It is a way of life.

2. Allow a few moments for the young people to ask questions of the speaker. You might also ask other leaders to share about some of the ways they have chosen to share Christ's light.

Poster Project

1. Gather the young people in small groups. Give each group a sheet of poster board, a ruler, pencils, and markers and explain the following process for creating a group poster:

Choose one symbol of light, such as the sun, a candle, or a flashlight. (Later you will have to explain why you chose one symbol over another.) Draw the symbol in the middle of the poster board.

In the center of the symbol, write five ways that you, as a group, can help spread the light of Christ. For example, you might invite new teens to join the youth group, volunteer as a group for a parish project, bake cookies together and take them to homebound parishioners, and so forth.

Around the outside of the symbol, draw three rays of light for each member of the small group. Ask each person to write three ways she or he can spread the light of Christ as an individual. Some examples include doing things the first time one is told, reaching out to someone at school who is alone a lot of the time, or taking time to talk to an elderly relative or neighbor.

2. After the groups have finished their poster, ask a spokesperson from each group to explain the symbol that they chose and some of the ideas that the group listed in the middle of the symbol. You might ask the rest of the group members to share at least one way that they plan to share the light.

3. Close the activity by encouraging the young people to put their strategies into action as soon as they can. By doing so they can really light up the world.

Letters to Parents

Note: This affirmation activity can be done even if the participants did not do the "Letters from Parents" activity.

Introduce this activity by making the following points in your own words:

Earlier in the retreat, everyone received a letter from some special people in their life. Now they have an opportunity to respond to those letters. Some people may find it difficult to talk to their parents. Putting feelings down on paper makes it easier to share them.

Write a love letter to your parents, describing ways they are they light of Christ in your family. If you have trouble getting started, you can think of some of the things your parents do or say that you are thankful for. You can say anything else you want to say to your parents, as long as it is honest and from the heart.

Distribute paper, envelopes, and pens or pencils, and ask the participants to go off to a place where they can be alone with their thoughts. Emphasize the need to respect other people's privacy. Encourage them to put some thought into their letter and to make it longer than a few sentences or a short paragraph.

Tell the teens to place their letter in the envelope when they are finished and address the envelope. Give them the option of taking their letter home and giving it to their parents, or giving the letters to you to mail.

Closing Prayer

Preparation. While the young people are writing their letters, set up for the closing prayer service. If possible, have the closing prayer in the church or a chapel, and include the Christmas lights that you used on the first day of the retreat. Be sure to include a Bible in the prayer space. Have available the candleholders and posters that the teens made earlier in the retreat and a wick or taper candle. If you have parish songbooks available, choose an opening and closing song.

Recruit a volunteer to read Jer. 1:4–10. Practice reading Matt. 5:14–16 so that you can proclaim it enthusiastically as good news. Memorize it if possible.

1. Distribute the candleholders to their owners. Using the lit pillar candle, lead the young people in a procession to the prayer space. Tell them to walk with their small group, and have someone from the group carry the poster that they created together. When you arrive in the prayer space, put the lit candle near the Bible. Tell the teens to sit with their group. Follow this order of service:

◎ If you chose music for the prayer, lead the group in the opening song.

◎ Invite the first reader to proclaim Jer. 1:4–10. Ask the young people to explain what the reading means to them in light of the retreat. Be sure to include a comment that age is not a factor in being a light of Christ in the world.

◎ One at a time, call each group forward with their poster and their candles. Have them read together the five ideas for group service that they listed in the middle of their symbol. When they have read the list, the other groups answer, "You are the light of the world." The small group responds with, "Lord, help us to share your light." Then each person lights her or his candle from the pillar candle and proceeds back to her or his seat, leaving the poster in the prayer space. Follow the same procedure with each small group.

◎ Proclaim Matt. 5:14–16. Pause at the end of each sentence and invite the teens to respond enthusiastically, "We are the light of the world!"

◎ If you chose music, close the prayer by leading the participants in song.

End the retreat by thanking the young people for their cooperation and encouraging them always to believe that they are indeed the light of Christ to the world and to live that truth.

(This retreat was developed by Maryann Hakowski, Yorktown, Virginia, a youth minister with more than eighteen years of experience.)

ALTERNATIVE APPROACHES

For part 3: We hold the light

◎ Depending on the time you have available on the first day, you may want to give the teens an extended break between the candleholder project and the closing prayer service. Provide board games, thought games, puzzles, and so forth.

For part 4: The Lord is my light and my salvation

◎ If the weather is good, consider doing the morning prayer outdoors. Begin the prayer by allowing the young people to lay in the grass, take in the beauty, and listen to the sounds around them.

◎ If you have an extended time period for the "Light and Sun Search," allow the participants to follow the same procedure with TV shows, movies, and books. Also, instead of sharing your own observations, ask the young people what they think the exercise had to do with letting one's light shine.

◎ In addition to a letter from each teen's parents, encourage parents to invite other family members to write letters: siblings, grandparents, godparents, and so forth. You might want to set a limit so that some people do not get a dozen letters while others get only two.

For part 5: Dimming the light of Christ

◎ If you have a priest available, plan a sacramental Reconciliation service on the theme of dimming the light of Christ in ourselves and others.

For part 6: We light the way for others

◎ Begin this section with a game that involves light, such as flashlight or laser tag, group shadow sculptures, or the old favorite, red light–green light.

◎ Instead of a prayer service, conclude the retreat with a eucharistic celebration using the same themes and readings.

After the retreat

◎ Follow the retreat with a surprise potluck dinner sponsored and attended by the families.

◎ Follow up on the posters the small groups created. Help them plan and execute at least one of their ideas for a group service project.

◎ Encourage the young people to let their light shine through prayer. During a follow-up session, ask them to write their own prayers. Publish them all together in a small booklet for the participants and other members of the parish.

◎ Plan a parent-teen night with social, educational, and spiritual activities for teens and parents to do together. Get the young people involved in the planning of the event. Consult the volume in the HELP series *Family Ideas for Ministry with Young Teens* for program suggestions.

NOTES

Use the space below to jot notes and reminders for the next time you use this retreat.

Let Your Light Shine

Write the answers to the following questions in your journal notebook.

✪ When and why have you wanted to be someone other than who you are?

✪ What are some of the things that you do really well?

✪ Name three specific ways that you can let your light shine. That is, how can you share your unique gifts and talents with others?

✪ Name three ways you can encourage other people—your family and friends— to let their light shine. That is, what gifts and talents do you see in other people that you would like them to share?

Christmas Island: A Parable of Light

Joseph and Mary Carpenter live in a comfortable home with their son on an island off the coast of Maine. They are surrounded by friends and loved by all their neighbors. But things were very different for them when they first moved to Christmas Island.

Joseph had become ill and could no longer do the work he had been doing for most of his adult life. He had to sell his business at the same time that Mary was expecting their baby. They decided to use most of their savings to move to Christmas Island and purchase a lighthouse on the coast of the island. But the people on the island hated the outsiders and treated them badly every time they came into town for supplies.

Joseph wanted to leave the lighthouse and get away from the town that was making him so miserable. He would have left, but Mary hesitated, insisting that their baby be born there—in the lighthouse. After that, she agreed that they could leave.

Joseph's illness grew worse. His body weakened and so did his spirit. He began to hate the people who treated him unfairly and the town around him. Then, on Christmas Eve, around midnight, his son was born, and Joseph was filled with such love and happiness that there was no longer any room in his heart for hatred. He wanted to tell the world of his happiness. So Joseph lit every lamp in every window of the lighthouse.

The next morning the news broadcast told of a near tragedy on that little island at midnight on Christmas Eve. A pilot, lost in the fog, was heading for a crash landing in the middle of the town, when the heavens lit up with a bright light in every direction. The pilot was able to get back on course and land his plane and his passengers safely.

Joseph's lights in the lighthouse windows had saved many people that night. But it was Joseph's light within himself—the light of God's love and forgiveness—that really saved the town. Because Joseph was able to let his light shine, he touched the lives of many people.

("Christmas Island" is adapted from a story by Mary Ellen Holmes that appeared in *The War Cry* [Christmas 1989].)

The Lord Is My Light and My Salvation

Adapted from Psalm 27

All. The Lord is my light and my salvation.

Group 1. The Lord is my light and my salvation;
   I will fear no one.
   The Lord protects me from all danger;
   I will never be afraid.

All. The Lord is my light and my salvation.

Group 2. I have asked the Lord for one thing;
   one thing only do I want:
   to live in the Lord's house all my life,
   to marvel there at God's goodness.

All. The Lord is my light and my salvation.

Group 1. Hear me, Lord, when I call to you!
   Be merciful and answer me!
   When you said, "Come worship me,"
   I answered, "I will come, Lord."

All. The Lord is my light and my salvation.

Group 2. I know that I will live to see God's goodness in this present life.
   Trust in the Lord.
   Have faith; do not despair.
   Trust in the Lord.

All. The Lord is my light and my salvation.

Closing Prayer

All. Dear Lord, thank you for being light in our darkness and for showing us the way to God. Help us to live in your light, to see your light
   in others, and to share your light with everyone we meet. Amen.

Dimming the Light of Christ

Spend some quiet time alone writing the answers to these questions in your journal notebook.

(@) What are some of the things that dim the light of Christ in people's life?

(@) Some of the ways the light of Christ is getting dimmer in my life are . . .
in my relationship with myself:
in my relationship with other people:
in my relationship with God:

(@) How can people keep the light of Christ from going out?

(@) Some ways that I can keep the light of Christ from going out in my life are . . .

(@) How can the sacrament of Reconciliation keep the light of Christ shining in people's life?

(@) When I think about the sacrament of Reconciliation,
I wonder about . . .
I remember that . . .
I plan to . . .

Beneath Our Masks

An Overnight Retreat on Being True to Oneself

This overnight retreat offers young teens an opportunity to explore the masks they wear that often get in the way of who they really are. It begins with the assumption that everyone tries to hide behind a mask at some point—even people who seem confident and self-assured. Together the young people examine their own false masks and discover ways to let their true self show.

Suggested Time

This retreat is designed as an overnight experience to allow time for community building and deeper sharing. The exact length of this retreat depends on how long the nutrition and recreation breaks are, how many mixers and games you use, and so forth.

Group Size

This retreat is most effective with groups of twenty or fewer. However, it can be done with any number of young people, divided into small groups, each led by an older teen or adult.

Special Considerations

This retreat plan presumes that the retreat will begin in the evening and end by midafternoon the next day. Parts 1, 2, and 3—from the name tag activity through the prayer on Psalm 139—happen on the first evening of the retreat. Parts 4 through 8 are designed for the second day. If you have a different schedule, you will need to adjust the plan accordingly to maintain the flow of the retreat.

Materials Needed

- ☼ 4-by-6-inch index cards, one for each participant
- ☼ a variety of colored markers
- ☼ newsprint
- ☼ safety pins, one for each participant
- ☼ copies of handout 1, "Name Treasure Hunt," one for each person
- ☼ pens or pencils
- ☼ a small prize (optional)
- ☼ paper plates, one for each person, with a hole punched on each side of the plate
- ☼ a hole punch
- ☼ 18-inch pieces of yarn or string, two for each person
- ☼ used magazines, stickers, and other craft supplies
- ☼ scissors, at least one for every two people
- ☼ glue sticks, at least one for every two people
- ☼ copies of handout 2, "Psalm 139," one for each person
- ☼ a pillar candle and matches
- ☼ masking tape
- ☼ a tape or CD player, and a recording of reflective music (optional)
- ☼ a tape or CD of an appropriate popular song about self-image, masks, or being true to yourself (optional)
- ☼ a 10-foot long piece of rope or string and two trees or poles (optional)
- ☼ tape, plastic, cardboard, 2-by-4-inch boards, or rope, to make a 3-foot square for each small group (optional)
- ☼ three 8½-by-11-inch pieces of cardboard (optional)
- ☼ one long piece of rope, string, masking tape, or adding machine tape
- ☼ two pieces of poster board
- ☼ a copy of resource 1, "Maskits," cut apart as scored

PROCEDURE

Part 1: Introduction and Community Building (40 to 50 minutes)

Preparation. Make a large sample name tag on newsprint, following the model below. Post the sample in the main retreat space.

Which cartoon character are you most like?	If you could be any person in history, who would you be?
NAME	
If you could be famous, what would you want to be known for?	If you could change your name, what would you change it to?

Fill in the names of the retreat participants on the left side of handout 1, and make a copy for each participant. You may need to add or delete lines, depending on the number of young people in the group.

1. As the young people arrive, give them each a 4-by-6-inch index card. Set out a variety of colored markers. Point out the sample name tag and ask them to make a personal name tag, answering the questions that are in each corner on the sample. Encourage them to decorate their name tag if time allows. Distribute safety pins so that the teens can fasten the name tag on their shirt when it is completed.

2. Welcome the participants to the retreat. If this is the first retreat experience for some, you may want to lead a short discussion around the following questions:

What is a retreat?

What do you think will happen on this retreat?

What do you hope will not happen?

Briefly explain the theme of the retreat and outline in a positive way the expectations that you have of the participants.

3. Use one of the following methods to form small groups, or find a method in section 1 of another book in the HELP series, *Community-Building Ideas for Ministry with Young Teens.*

Option 1: Counting off

Add a variation to this traditional method of forming groups. Instead of using numbers to count off, use common phrases or titles such as the following:

◎ to form three groups: "snap, crackle, pop" or "vanilla, chocolate, strawberry"

◎ to form four groups: "head, shoulders, knees, toes" or "eenie, meenie, miney, moe"

◎ to form five groups: "Won't you be my neighbor?" or *"A, E, I, O, U"*

Option 2: Making a pizza

Decide how many people you want in each small group. Then write or type on a blank piece of paper the same number of pizza ingredients from the following list: dough, sauce, cheese, pepperoni, sausage, mushrooms, olives, peppers, anchovies. Make enough copies of the list so that everyone gets one ingredient. Cut the ingredients list apart, mix the ingredients up in a bag, and distribute them randomly. Explain to the participants that they will form groups by "making pizzas." You may want to list the required ingredients on a sheet of newsprint so that the teens know what the groups should include.

Option 3: Assigned groups

If you know who the retreat participants are ahead of time, establish the groups before the retreat. This method gives you control over who is in each group. Use different colored index cards for each group's name tags.

4. Explain that each person has 30 seconds to share the contents of her or his name tag with the small group, beginning with the person who has the most letters in her or his first and last names. Instead of simply answering the questions, the participants are to explain why they wrote what they did. Encourage the other participants to ask clarifying questions.

While this is happening, put copies of handout 1, and pens or pencils near each group, to be distributed at the appropriate time.

5. Ask someone in each group to distribute a copy of handout 1, and a pen or pencil to each person. Invite the young people to try to get to know something about everyone on the retreat. Explain that the handout will help them accomplish that goal. Between now and the end of the retreat, they are to fill in the required information about each participant. You may want to offer a small prize to the person who completes the handout first (without copying someone else's answers, that is!)

Give them a few minutes to fill in the answers for the members of their small group before moving on to part 2.

Note. Depending on your time frame and the needs of your group, you may want to engage the small groups in some bonding activities. The more comfortable the young people feel with one another, the more likely they are to share their thoughts. You can find a number of ideas in *Community-Building Ideas for Ministry with Young Teens* (HELP series, Saint Mary's Press, 2001); *Building Community in Youth Groups,* by Denny Rydberg (Loveland, CO: Group Publishing, 1985); and *Youth Group Trust Builders,* also by Denny Rydberg (Loveland, CO: Group Publishing, 1993).

Part 2: We All Wear Masks (45 to 60 minutes)

Preparation. Make a paper-plate mask as described in step 2 to demonstrate what you are looking for in this exercise.

Punch each paper plate with two holes, one on the left edge and the other directly across from it on the right edge.

1. Make the following comments in your own words, adding your own thoughts to set the theme of the retreat:

Young children have no need to be anyone but who they are. They are accepted and loved by everyone in their world. Their behavior is sometimes challenged, but the person who they are is celebrated and cherished.

As they grow, people have experiences that lead them to believe that they are not lovable. They believe that they do not have what it takes to fit in with their peer group. So in order to be accepted, they try to change who they are. They hide behind false masks that they think will earn them respect and acceptance. They want to be someone that they are not.

Often the face people show to the world is very different from the face they hide inside. They are hesitant to show how they really feel, for fear that others will ridicule them or not respect their feelings.

Sometimes masks can be helpful in getting through a situation. They help people see that they can, in fact, do things they did not think were possible. For example, if a person is nervous about giving a speech in class, a mask of self-confidence and control could allow that person to experience success.

However, masks sometimes cover the parts of a person that are good and true. They often make people say and do things that do not put forth their best self.

The purpose of this retreat is to explore some of the masks we wear and to discover ways to be our true self.

2. Distribute a paper plate and two 18-inch pieces of string or yarn to each person. Make available to each small group a variety of markers, stickers, magazines, scissors, glue sticks, and so forth. Announce that each person will

create his or her own "outside-inside" mask. Use the mask that you created before the retreat as an example, and explain the project as follows:

Begin by cutting out holes for your eyes. Then decorate the front of the mask with words, pictures, drawings, stickers, and other things that represent how you would like to appear to others. This is your "outside" mask.

On the reverse side of your mask, again use words, pictures, drawings, stickers, and anything else that represents how you really feel. Be sure to include the negative feelings that you try to hide as well as the positive ones that you do not show because you are afraid of being ridiculed. This is your "inside" mask. When you finish, tie a piece of string or yarn to each hole.

Ask the participants to respect one another's privacy, particularly when they are doing their inside mask. You may want to suggest that they move to a private spot when they get to that part of the project. Allow 20 to 30 minutes for the young people to work on their masks.

3. Invite the participants to share their outside mask with others in their small group. Encourage the group members to ask clarifying questions and make constructive comments. Do not have them share their inside mask at this time.

Nutrition and Recreation Break

Part 3: Prayer (30 to 60 minutes)

Preparation. During the break set up a prayer space with a candle, a Bible, and whatever else you have to create a reflective atmosphere.

1. Gather the young people in their small groups once again. Give each small group a sheet of newsprint and some markers. Introduce the exercise by noting that no matter what masks we wear, God always sees and loves the person that we really are. A biblical writer who was well aware of God's constant love and care wrote a psalm about it. Read aloud Psalm 139:1–10,13–14,23–24.

2. Distribute copies of handout 2. Explain that as a group, they are to rewrite the psalm in a language that speaks to people their age living in their community and going to their schools. They are to write their finished product on newsprint. Set a time limit of 20 to 30 minutes.

3. When all groups have finished the task, move to the prayer space. Tell the participants to bring their masks, and ask the group leaders to bring their group's version of Psalm 139. Direct the participants to sit around the candle,

and the leaders to post the psalms. Give the young people a chance to look over the psalms, but do not read the paraphrases at this time.

Light the candle and, if possible, dim the lights. If you cannot dim the lights, turn off a few, leaving only enough light for the group leaders to read. If you have reflective music available, begin playing it at this time.

Invite the young people to close their eyes and listen to the sounds in the room. When everyone is settled, ask them to put on their mask, this time with the inside out. This should be done quietly and reverently. Ask them to respect everyone's privacy by not looking around to see what people put on their inside mask.

When everyone is quiet, make the following points in your own words:

The side of the mask that is facing out is the side we usually try to hide from others. We may try to hide our fears, our insecurities, and our doubts. We may try to hide that we take joy in certain things, like seeing a baby or being with our family. We might even try to hide things about ourselves that we're proud of.

But this is the side of us that God sees. And no matter what is on our inside mask, that is, what is in our heart, God knows about it and loves us. God challenges us to move beyond some of the things that prevent us from being our best self. But in spite of those things, God loves us. Nothing we can ever do will cut us off from God's love.

Another challenge that God places before us is to allow other people to be who they really are. When we put people down or ridicule them, we force them to wear their outside mask, even though it may not always be their true self. We owe it to one another to be true to the self God created us to be and to value that truth in others.

4. Begin reading Psalm 139 from handout 2. Pause for a few seconds, then invite the group leaders to take turns reading their group's paraphrase. Pause a few seconds between each version.

Invite the group leaders to untie the mask of every young person in their small group. As they do so, encourage them to say something like, "Be true to yourself. Be true to your God."

5. Pass the candle around the group. Invite each person to complete the statement, "I believe . . ." as it applies to themselves, their God, or God's relationship with the world. Assure them that if they would rather not say anything, they do not have to. They should just hold the candle for a few seconds, then pass it to the next person.

You may want to start this process with one of the group leaders or a young person you know is likely to say something. This will set the tone for the rest of the group.

6. Close with a spontaneous prayer thanking God for making us who we are and for loving us no matter what. If you have an appropriate popular song on the theme of self-image, masks, or being true to oneself, play it at this time.

Note: This outline presumes that the first day of the retreat ends here. If your schedule is different, you may want to provide a meal and an extended recreation break at this time.

Part 4: Prayer and Group Problem Solving (60 to 120 minutes)

Preparation. Decide which of the activities you will use from the three outlined below. Set up the game areas with the proper equipment, depending on which activities you use.

1. Gather the participants in small groups. Give each group a sheet of newsprint and some markers. Announce that they will work together to create a morning prayer. Each person in the group will add one word at a time to create phrases, sentences, and finally, a whole prayer.

Begin with the person in each group who has the youngest sibling and move around the circle to that person's right. Go around the circle three to five times, depending on the size of the group. Three times will be plenty if the group is large.

2. After each group has completed its prayer, share the prayers with everyone. Conclude the morning prayer with a spontaneous prayer of your own, thanking God for the gift of a new day.

3. If possible, conduct the following part of the retreat outdoors. If that is not possible, move to a gym or another wide open space on the retreat site.

Explain that just as the small groups worked together to write a prayer, they will now work together to solve some problems. Emphasize that these activities are not competitions between groups. Rather, they provide a chance to see one another's true colors and to let their own colors shine. Encourage them to work together to solve the problem and to listen to, respect, and observe one another.

Lead the group in one or more of the following activities.

Climbing the Walls

Preparation. This strategy involves creating the effect of a wall that is about four feet high. You can do this by running a string between two trees, two poles, or similar stationary objects. The space under the string does not have to be filled.

Tell the groups to stand together on one side of their wall. When everyone is in place, explain the following directions:

The group's task is to get everyone over the rope wall safely. No one can go under the rope or around the sides. Avoid touching the rope at all.

No one can get herself or himself over the wall. That is, no hurdling or high jumping is allowed.

If someone who made it over the wall wants to go back and help someone else get over the wall, he or she must be helped back over the wall to the starting side and then go over again.

Emphasize the need to pay attention to safety issues. Be sure to have an adult with each group to act as a spotter. Also point out once again that this activity is not a competition. It is a problem-solving activity. So nothing is to be gained by the group that finishes first.

(This activity is adapted from Denny Rydberg, *Building Community in Youth Groups,* pp. 36–37.)

Stand in the Square

Preparation. Mark off a 3-foot square on the ground for each small group. Use tape, plastic, cardboard, 2-by-4-inch boards, rope, or whatever else works in your setting. If the groups consist of six or fewer people, reduce the size of the square to 2 1/2 feet.

Gather each small group around a square. Explain that each group's task is to get every member in the square. Suggest that they try to accomplish that goal now. They will likely all huddle into the square with little trouble. Affirm their efforts, then announce that because it was so easy for them, you are imposing a new rule: Each group can have only two feet touching the ground. This means that in a group of eight people, only two of their sixteen feet may be on the ground. The group must be able to hold that position for 10 seconds.

When you are certain that the teens understand the task, tell them to begin. They should not rush to be first. Instead, they should look for the most creative way to solve the problem.

Swamp Crossing

Preparation. Mark off a swamp for each group by placing two pieces of rope or two 2-by-4-inch boards on the ground 10 to 12 feet apart. Put three pieces of cardboard, about 8 1/2-by-11 inches each, near one end of each swamp.

Explain the following situation:

Your group is on a journey. You have come to a swamp that is infested with hungry alligators that have not eaten in days, and you must find a way to get everyone in your group across. The only way to cross safely is to use the three alligator shields that are at the beginning of the swamp. You must follow certain rules:

Only one foot or other body part may be on an alligator shield at one time.

Any body part that is not on a shield and touches the water will get consumed immediately by an alligator. You cannot use this body part for the rest of the exercise. If your entire body falls into the water, you must start over from the beginning.

The shields may be picked up and moved to get people across, but they may not be thrown or slid across the water.

When you are sure that the young people understand the directions, signal them to start. Emphasize that this is an exercise to see who can come up with a creative solution to the problem. It is not a competition to see who finishes first.

(This activity is adapted from Denny Rydberg, *Building Community in Youth Groups,* pp. 48–49.)

You may want to provide refreshments and a break for the young people at this time, especially if you used all three activities.

4. Process the problem-solving activities in small groups using the following questions.
◎ Who in the group came up with creative ideas to solve the problem?
◎ Which ideas worked? Which didn't?
◎ What did it take to solve the problem?
◎ What did you notice about someone in the group that you had never noticed or paid attention to before?
◎ What did you find out about yourself?
◎ What do these problem-solving activities have to do with the theme of this retreat?

5. Gather the participants into one large group. Ask them to share some of the discussion that went on in their small groups, particularly their answers to the last question. Close this part of the retreat by affirming the problem-solving skills of the teens, their willingness to work together, and their attentiveness to the true colors of other people.

Nutrition and Recreation Break

Part 5: Beneath Our Masks (20 to 35 minutes)

Preparation. Create a continuum along the floor, long enough to provide a place for everyone in the group to stand. Use string, rope, masking tape, or adding machine tape. At one end of the continuum, post a sign that says "Rough and tough." On the other end, post a sign that says "Tender care."

1. Gather the young people on one side of the continuum. Begin this activity by making the following comments in your own words:

People wear masks for all kinds of reasons, but usually our masks are a reaction to the way we have been treated by ourselves, other people, and the world in general. Masks are our way of shielding ourselves from being ridiculed, hurt, or made to feel like we do not measure up.

If a person is treated with tender care by everyone, he or she has no need for masks. If a person is treated roughly, the natural human reaction is to protect oneself. That protection might take the form of a mask.

2. Announce that you will read a few situations that most teens are likely to be in during the week. You want them to move to a point on the continuum that represents how they were treated by that person or group during the past week. If they were treated with respect—affirmed for who they are and what they do but challenged to grow—and generally felt positive about their interaction with that person or group, they should move to the side that says "Tender care." Ask the teens to offer examples that might fall into the category of being treated with tender care.

If they were hurt, ridiculed, or somehow made to feel inadequate, they should move to the side that says "Rough and tough." Encourage the young people to offer examples that might fall into the category of being treated in this manner.

Point out that it is likely that most people's experience will be somewhere between the two ends. In those cases, they are to move to a point on the continuum that sums up their experience that week.

Present the following situations, and allow time for the young people to move. If you think that the teens will be open, you may want to invite volunteers to share why they chose the place on the continuum that they did.

In the past week . . .

how were you treated by your family?

how were you treated by your friends?

how were you treated by your teachers?

how were you treated by your peers?

how were you treated by your coaches and teammates?

how did you treat yourself?

3. Invite the teens to think about the mask that they created earlier in the retreat. Raise the following questions, but do not invite the teens to voice their answers. Just give them a few seconds to think.

Which words, phrases, and symbols on your outside mask are a result of the way you have been treated?

Which words, phrases, and symbols on your inside mask represent how you really felt in each situation?

Part 6: Behind Our Masks (45 to 60 minutes)

1. Gather the young people in their small groups. Announce that each group will get a scenario. They are to come up with a snapshot skit that represents and then interprets the situation. You may need to give an example like the following:

Karla is an intelligent girl and kind of shy. She doesn't mingle much with others, but she does have one or two close friends. She spends a lot of time alone. People see Karla as a geek, a snob, and a loner. They do not treat her well, and sometimes they just leave her alone. She seems to like it that way.

The group's task is to do a 60-second skit that depicts Karla and her classmates at school on a typical day. After 60 seconds the actors freeze, as if someone took a snapshot. Then someone from the scene unfreezes and explains what Karla's outside mask is (quiet, loner, snob, socially challenged, and so forth). Someone else from the scene unfreezes and explains what Karla's inside mask might look like (lonely, shy, low self-esteem, afraid, wishes she could be someone else, and so forth).

2. Sum up the directions in this way:

Someone from the group chooses a scenario and reads it to the group.

Together the group members come up with an idea for a skit that lasts no more than 60 seconds. They also name what the main character's outside mask is and try to determine why the person is like he or she is, or what that character's inside mask is like.

The group performs the skit and freezes after 60 seconds.

One person unfreezes and tells about the character's outside mask.

Another person unfreezes and explains what the character's inside mask might look like.

3. Ask the small groups to determine which person in the group has the most pets. That person should come to you and select one of the scenarios from resource 1. Allow about 15 minutes for the groups to prepare their presentation. You might want to caution the group leaders not to let anyone be typecast, in order to maintain emotional safety for all the participants. In other words, someone who has to deal with the label of "geek" in real life should be spared from playing the role in the skit.

4. When the groups are ready, invite them to perform for one another. After they are finished describing the outside and inside masks of the main character, solicit additional feedback from the rest of the group. Discuss with them the reasons the character chooses to wear the outside mask that he or she wears.

Close the activity by emphasizing once again that people's outward appearances do not always reflect what they feel on the inside.

Nutrition and Recreation Break

Part 7: We All Play a Part (25 to 35 minutes)

1. Do the following reflection in small groups. If your space is tight, you may want to move to a space where the groups can spread out a little more.

Direct the young people to stand in a tight circle with their small-group members, facing in, shoulders touching. Tell them that you will read a few statements. If they have ever had that experience, they should follow the direction you give after the statement. Request that they do this in silence.

When they are quiet, begin reading the following statements, pausing in between each until the young people perform the appropriate action:

If you have ever tried to be someone you're not, close your eyes and keep them closed.

If you have ever excluded someone just because he or she wasn't part of your group of friends, take a step back.

If you have ever been mean to a peer or family member, take another step back.

If you have ever called someone by a name that hurt them, take another step back.

If you have ever ridiculed someone because of that person's size, shape, or ability, turn around and face out of the circle.

If you have ever ignored someone you did not want to be associated with, extend your arms. Keep them in that position.

When you extend your arms, you are all alone. You cannot touch anyone else or lean on anyone. Sometimes our treatment of other people isolates them and us. They are forced to be someone they are not in order to keep from getting torn down. And after a while, life begins to hurt—much as your arms are beginning to hurt by now. But because we were created by God for goodness, we have also had experiences of building other people up. So . . .

If you have ever said something nice to a person just because, put your arms down.

If you have ever given a sincere compliment to someone who was not used to receiving compliments, turn back into the circle.

If you have ever defended someone who was being ridiculed by others, take a step forward.

If you have ever reached out to someone who seemed to be all alone, take a step forward.

If you have ever included someone who was not a regular part of your group in something that you and your friends were doing, take a step forward.

If you have ever looked behind someone's outside mask to try to get to know that person, open your eyes.

If you have ever let anyone else see behind your outside mask, stretch out your arms and rest them on your neighbor's shoulders.

It is much more comfortable to stretch out your arms when you have the support of other people than it was when you were all alone. Being who we are and treating one another in a way that allows them to be true to themselves creates a supportive environment in which people can be all that God meant them to be.

(Adapted from Thom and Joani Schultz, *Do It! Active Learning in Youth Ministry,* pp. 65–67)

2. Give each small group a sheet of newsprint and some markers. Explain that they are to write a group creed, that is, statements of belief and promises of action they all agree on that can serve as guiding principles. They are to come up with one or two belief statements and one or two accompanying action statements. You may want to provide simple sentence starters, such as the following:

We believe . . .

And because of this belief, we will . . .

Allow about 15 minutes for the groups to complete the task.

Part 8: Closing Prayer (15 minutes)

Preparation. Recreate the prayer space as you had it for the Psalm 139 prayer, including the paraphrases of the psalm that the groups wrote.

1. Invite the small-group leaders to bring their statements of beliefs and actions and post them in the prayer space. The young people should bring the masks they created earlier in the retreat.

Light the candle and play reflective music if you have it available. Ask the participants to put on their masks and sit quietly. Suggest that they reread their paraphrases of Psalm 139.

2. Summarize the retreat by making the following comments in your own words:

Underneath the mask of every person lies the face of Jesus. No matter what we look like, dress like, what our abilities or weaknesses are, we are all children of God, created in God's image to reflect God's love. What would the world be like if we all wore the face of Jesus and saw that face on others?

3. Invite each of the young teens to take off the mask of one other person. As they do so, they are to say "[Name], I see the face of Jesus in you." Then have them place the mask around the candle, inside facing up.

When everyone's mask is removed, ask the teens to stand in a circle. Together have them read their group's belief and action statements.

4. Thank the young people for their enthusiasm, hard work, playful spirit, and cooperation during the retreat. Close the retreat by reading Phil. 4:8–9.

(The concept and many of the ideas for this retreat came from Ruthie Nonnenkamp, Holy Trinity Parish, Louisville, Kentucky.)

ALTERNATIVE APPROACHES

For part 1: Introduction and community building

◎ If all the young people arrive at the same time, consider having them make name tags for one another. Use an objective method to create pairs. For example, cut candy bar wrappers or other snack packages in half. Distribute the halves randomly among the teens. Announce that they are to form pairs by finding the match to their wrapper.

◎ Give each small group a sheet of newsprint. Have the members brainstorm some basic ground rules for the retreat. When all the groups have completed the task, post them and share them with the whole group. Be sure the list includes rules about listening respectfully, not putting people down, promptness, and safety.

For part 2: We all wear masks

◎ Have the participants make their outside mask as scheduled and share it with the group. Direct them to do the reverse side as part of the prayer that follows:

Provide homemade chocolate-chip cookies for snack time, preferably warm from the oven. Just before the break, give each small group a plate of cookies and a napkin. Announce that each person should take a cookie, examine it, and then place it on the napkin. Direct the leaders to turn away from the participants and mix up the cookies on the napkin. Then challenge the teens to find their own cookie. While they are eating their cookie, ask the young people to respond to this question: "How are chocolate-chip cookies like people?" Affirm them as they share their answers. Sum up the discussion by making the following points:

◎ Like chocolate-chip cookies, some people have more dough, some more chips, their chips are arranged differently, and so forth. But no matter what the cookies look like, they are all wonderful. It's almost impossible to make a bad chocolate-chip cookie.

Continue with the scheduled break.

For part 3: Prayer

◎ If your time is limited, eliminate the paraphrasing exercise. Simply move the young people into their small groups after the break and continue with the prayer.

◎ If your schedule does not call for ending the day with this prayer, you may simply want to have the small groups share their own paraphrase of Psalm 139 with the large group. Then move on to a break or to the next section.

◎ A more active way to do the paraphrase exercise is to group the young people in pairs, cut the psalm into phrases or verses, and give each pair one of the phrases or verses. Also give each pair a long, narrow strip of paper, about 24-by-4 inches. Invite them to paraphrase their line and write it on the paper. Create the new psalm by taping the paraphrased lines to the wall or to a sheet of butcher paper.

◎ Use the classic children's story *The Runaway Bunny* as part of the prayer. The story tells about a young rabbit who threatens to run away and change himself in order to distance himself from his mother. The mother rabbit vows to stay with him and change herself to always be close to him. It is a fitting image of God and complements Psalm 139.

For part 4: Prayer and group problem solving

◎ For the sake of efficiency, you may want to rotate the groups through the activities, setting up as many stations as needed to have all the groups occupied for the duration of the period.

◎ For more options see *Community-Building Ideas for Ministry with Young Teens* in the HELP series); *Building Community in Youth Groups,* by Denny Rydberg; and *Youth Group Trust Builders,* also by Denny Rydberg.

For part 5: Beneath our masks

◎ If you do not think that the young people will be open and honest in sharing this kind of information by moving on the continuum, create a handout that they can do privately.

◎ Add other situations that might apply in the continuum exercise, such as the parish community, the media, the local community, adults in their life that are not family, and so forth.

For part 6: Behind our masks

◎ To avoid confusion, you may want to post the skit directions on newsprint or give a copy to each small-group leader.

For part 7: We all play a part

◎ If you have time and your group is willing, offer the teens the opportunity to write a letter of apology to someone whom they have excluded, ridiculed, or otherwise hurt. Give them the chance to send it if they wish. If they do not want to send it, encourage them to hold on to it and read it periodically, resolving again to treat everyone with respect and dignity.

◎ Type up the group statements of belief and action after the retreat and send a copy to every teen. Encourage them to post it in a place where they will see it frequently, such as their bedroom mirror, locker, or notebook.

◎ Consider adding an affirmation exercise to the retreat. Direct everyone to make a new mask and put their name on it. Pass the masks around the group, and have the participants write authentically affirming statements on everyone's mask.

For part 8: Closing prayer

◎ If your group is small, do the unmasking ritual one person at a time. Have someone come up to the prayer space. Take that person's mask off while saying " [Name], I see the face of Jesus in you." Place the mask in the prayer space, then ask the next person to come up. The newly unmasked person removes the mask of the second person. Continue until everyone's mask is removed.

◎ If your group is small, replace the scriptural reading with Rom. 12:9–18. Insert the names of the young people in between the phrases. Be sure to include everyone.

NOTES

Use the space below to jot notes and reminders for the next time you use this retreat.

Name Treasure Hunt

Over the course of this retreat, answer the following questions about each person in the group.

Retreatants' Names

_____ would like to be famous for _____

_____ would like to be this person from history _____

because _____

_____ would prefer the name _____

_____ is most like the cartoon character _____

because _____

_____ would like to be famous for _____

_____ would like to be this person from history _____

because _____

_____ would prefer the name _____

_____ is most like the cartoon character _____

because _____

_____ would like to be famous for _____

_____ would like to be this person from history _____

because _____

_____ would prefer the name _____

_____ is most like the cartoon character _____

because _____

_____ would like to be famous for _____

_____ would like to be this person from history _____

because _____

_____ would prefer the name _____

_____ is most like the cartoon character _____

because _____

Psalm 139

O LORD, you have searched me and known me.
You know when I sit down and when I rise up;
    you discern my thoughts from far away.
You search out my path and my lying down,
    and are acquainted with all my ways.
Even before a word is on my tongue,
    O LORD, you know it completely.
You hem me in, behind and before,
    and lay your hand upon me.
Such knowledge is too wonderful for me;
    it is so high that I cannot attain it.

Where can I go from your spirit?
    Or where can I flee from your presence.
If I ascend to heaven, you are there;
    if I make my bed in Sheol, you are there.
If I take the wings of the morning
    and settle at the farthest limits of the sea,
even there your hand shall lead me,
    and your right hand shall hold me fast.

· · · · · · · · · · · · · ·

For it was you who formed my inward parts;
    you knit me together in my mother's womb.
I praise you, for I am fearfully and wonderfully made.
    Wonderful are your works;
that I know very well.

· · · · · · · · · · · · · ·

Search me, O God, and know my heart;
    test me and know my thoughts.
See if there is any wicked way in me,
    and lead me in the way everlasting.
(Ps. 139:1–10,13–14, 23–24)

Maskits

Make a photocopy of this resource and cut it apart as scored. Choose the scenarios that you think will work best with your group.

Trent is bigger than just about anyone else in his class. He plays football and is pretty good at it. He works hard and has won the respect of his coach and teammates. But he never really seems to come off the football field. At school he is always bullying people, being mean, and acting up in class. People who know him well say that he is very different at home, where he is the oldest of three children. His parents often rely on him to take care of his seven-year-old brother and three-year-old sister.

Alicia is gorgeous. There is no other word for it. All the girls know it; all the guys know it. The trouble is, Alicia doesn't know it. Or at least she doesn't believe it. She's always fussing about her looks, and calling herself fat, ugly, and dumb. She's kind of loud; you always know when Alicia is around. She's a B student at school and a pretty good softball player. She's always saying how jealous she is of this person because of her grades or of that person because of his easy way of being with people.

To listen to Jerome on Monday morning one would think that he spent all weekend at wild parties. He brags about how much he drank and how far he got with certain girls. He says that he wants to have sex with sixteen different girls by the time he's sixteen. You were on a bike ride with some friends last weekend, and you saw Jerome and his family fishing at the pier. He didn't see you, though. Jerome's parents are both small and slender, as are Jerome and his sister, who is just a year younger. You almost didn't recognize Jerome at first. He and his sister look a lot alike. They both wear glasses, their hair is the same length, and their bodies even look kind of similar.

Karla is an intelligent girl and kind of shy. She doesn't mingle much with others, but she does have one or two close friends. She spends a lot of time alone. People see Karla as a geek, a snob, and a loner. They do not treat her well, and sometimes they just leave her alone. She seems to like it that way.

Angela has always been very bright. She read whole books in kindergarten. She was in the weekly challenge group for fourth and fifth graders who were academically gifted. She had her heart set on being an astronaut. She always won the award for the highest grades at the end of the year. Needless to say, teachers really liked her. Everyone knew it. But things changed in middle school. Lately Angela has been quiet in class. She doesn't always get the highest grade on tests anymore, and sometimes she comes to school without her homework. Last week, for the first time in her life, she got a C on a math test. She just laughed it off. In fact, she was almost proud of it.

Everything is a joke to Matt. He's always the life of the party, the class clown, the person everyone likes to sit near at a school assembly—or any other time for that matter. He can make even the most depressed person smile. Nothing seems to get him down. Nothing. Not his parents' divorce, not missing the cut for the soccer team, not his grandfather's cancer, not having the bike that he paid for with his own hard-earned money stolen. Nothing gets Matt down. In fact, sometimes his carefree attitude gets a little annoying.

Chad is a pain in the neck. He seems to enjoy annoying people—especially teachers, coaches, or anybody in authority. I don't know why he comes to youth group. He just sits there and doesn't do anything or say anything, except to make snide remarks or ridicule someone. He gets some of the other guys involved in his antics, too. He's gotten sent home a few times when the adult leaders had their fill of him. But he keeps coming back. The youth leader talked to his parents. They know he's a problem, and they know that Chad needs help. But they both have responsible jobs and work long hours, so getting Chad someplace means that one of them has to take time off.

Janine is fairly new to the school. She was in a boarding school for a couple years while her parents were traveling. Janine affects most people like fingernails on a chalkboard. She's whiny, snobbish, and thinks she's better than everyone else. She hardly ever wears the same outfit twice. She complains that none of the stores in the area have anything she would even consider wearing. Her parents are wealthy, and they occasionally take Janine to New York or Chicago for a shopping trip. Whatever friends she has, she manages to turn them against her.

Called by Name
A Confirmation Retreat

OVERVIEW

This retreat is best suited to a group of young teens that is preparing for the sacrament of Confirmation. It explores the themes of wind, fire, and water as a way of focusing on the commitment to be a disciple of Christ in the world and an active member of the Catholic community.

Suggested Time

This retreat can be done in 5 to 7 hours, depending on the size of the group and the number and length of breaks that you schedule.

Group Size

This retreat is most effective with groups of twenty or fewer. However, it can be done with any number of young people, divided into small groups, each led by an older teen or adult.

Materials Needed

- ☼ name tags
- ☼ newsprint and markers
- ☼ masking tape
- ☼ a pillar candle and matches
- ☼ a tape or CD player, and a recording of reflective music (optional)
- ☼ poster board, two sheets for each small group

- pens or pencils
- copies of handout 1, "Dear God," one for each person
- Bibles, one for each person
- copies of resource 1, "Scriptural Puzzle," one for each group, cut apart as scored
- a bowl of water
- a branch
- a variety of props (optional)
- copies of handout 2, "The Beginning," one for each person (optional)
- copies of handout 3, "Prayer for the Gifts of the Spirit," one for each person
- four copies of resource 2, "Our Statement of Belief"
- four small bowls of bath oil or olive oil

PROCEDURE

Part 1: Getting Started (55 to 65 minutes)

Introduction and Group Building

Preparation. Assign each participant to one of four groups: earth, wind, water, or fire. Create a name tag for each person that designates which group he or she is in. You may want to create construction-paper symbols of the four groups or simply use stick-on name tags with different-colored borders to designate each group. Leave plenty of room around the person's name for things that will be added later in the retreat.

Set up chairs in a circle around a central table that will be used as a prayer space. If possible, the table should be circular. Place a pillar candle on the table.

1. As the young people arrive, give each of them a name tag and ask them to be seated in the circle. You may want to provide some interim activities to pass the time until everyone has arrived. Check another book in the HELP series, *Community-Building Ideas for Ministry with Young Teens,* for suggestions.

Welcome everyone to the retreat. Introduce yourself and the other leaders by stating your name and explaining if you are more like earth, wind, water, or fire, and why. Invite each leader to introduce herself or himself in the same way. Two examples follow here:

My name is _____. I am more like earth because I am steady and reliable.

My name is _____. I am more like wind because I move around a lot.

2. Once all the leaders have been introduced, invite the young people to gather in their small groups according to their name tags. Give each small group two sheets of newsprint and some markers. Explain that in their small groups they are to briefly introduce themselves. Then, as a group, they are to complete the following statements according to the name of their group:

People who are like _____ [earth, water, wind, or fire] are

_____ .

God is like _____ [earth, water, wind, or fire] because _____ .

As a group they are to come up with as many answers to the two sentence-starters as they can.

Allow about 5 minutes for the small groups to work together. When time is up, ask the groups to share their results. Post the results somewhere in the room.

Group Scrabble

1. Announce that the groups will engage in a friendly game of Scrabble. Instead of game pieces, they will use themselves. Each group is to come up with the longest word they can possibly spell using only one letter of each person's first name. In other words, if the group consists of eight people, the longest word they can possibly make will be eight letters long, using only one letter from each person's name.

If the groups have different numbers of members, use the names of leaders to even things out. Allow a few minutes for the groups to come up with their word.

2. Tell the young people to spell the word by arranging themselves in order. Each group should spell its word by having each member call out his or her letter.

Repeat the process as many times as your schedule and the young people's interest allows.

Opening Prayer

1. Gather the young people around the prayer table. Light the candle. Ask the teens to close their eyes and be silent for a few moments. If you are using reflective music, begin playing it at this time. Then say something like the following in your own words, pausing after each phrase to give the young people a chance to focus:

Listen to the sounds in the room. . . . Listen to the beating of your own heart. . . . Feel the movement of the air in the room . . . on your face . . . on your hands. . . . Pay attention to your breathing. . . . Try to slow it down and breathe more deeply. . . . We are in the presence of something—and someone—sacred.

Pause for a minute and let the silence settle. Then pray the following prayer, or create one spontaneously on the same themes.

Creator God, we ask the blessings of your Spirit, the Holy Spirit of Jesus, upon us as we come together to listen to your voice in our life. May this Spirit find a welcome place in our heart. May it open our mind and our eyes to see ourselves and this world as you see it. May this Holy Spirit of Jesus open our ears that we may hear you calling us by name, challenging us to share your love with all. In the name of Jesus we pray. Amen.

Introduction to the Retreat

1. Invite the young people to explain what a retreat is. You might want to ask the following questions:

Why do people go on retreat?

Why would we want to do this before Confirmation?

What do you think will happen today?

What do you hope will not happen today?

2. Address their concerns, affirm their comments, and make the following points in your own words:

A retreat is a sacred time, a time for taking a long, hard look at ourselves and the world around us. It is a time for sharing stories and secrets. It is a time for putting things in order. It is also a time to be with good people and to make good memories.

This retreat is part of a special time in your life, part of your preparation for Confirmation. We will be doing a lot and thinking about many things. We hope that you will learn something about yourself and about this step that you are about to take in your life.

Part 2: Wind, Spirit, and the Breath of God (60 to 75 minutes)

Small-Group Activity: We Are More

Preparation. Recruit three people to read the following scriptural passages:
◎ Gen. 1:1–2
◎ Gen. 2:7
◎ Gen. 1:27

1. Direct the young people to gather with their small group. Distribute a sheet of poster board and a variety of markers to each group. Tell them to write the words, "We are . . ." at the top of the poster board. Underneath they are to write nouns and adjectives that describe who they are. For example, their poster might include the following:

eighth graders
bike riders
Catholic
New Yorkers
Mexican Americans

Encourage them to fill their poster with words or names that describe them. They can use words that describe what they have in common or what sets them apart from one another. Tell them to circle the words that are characteristics of some people in the group but not others. Allow about 5 minutes for this activity. After everyone is done, have the groups compare their posters.

2. Affirm the teens for their creative posters. Then explain that according to God, we are much more than most of us think we are. In each of us, there is something mysterious. It is a part of us that we do not always talk about. It is a part of us that is so deep that we do not fully understand it.

Call the three volunteers that you recruited before the session to read aloud the scriptural passages:

◎ Gen. 1:1–2
◎ Gen. 2:7
◎ Gen. 1:27

Direct the small groups to turn their poster over, write at the top, "We are more!" and then come up with words and phrases that God might use to describe them. Give examples like the following:

holy
mysterious
fearfully, wonderfully made
children of God
disciples of Jesus

Again, encourage them to fill up the poster with words and phrases that describe who they are in God's eyes. Allow about 5 minutes for them to fill the poster. When they are finished, invite them to take turns reading the words and phrases on their group's poster, beginning each with, "We are . . ."

When each group has read its poster, ask the members if they can circle anything on this side that is unique to only a few people in the group, as they did on the other side of the poster. It should become apparent that the words and phrases on the back side of the poster apply to everyone.

Make the following points in your own words:

The names we give to people or things and the qualities we assign to them are important because they tell us about how we are related to one another. A name can be a blessing or a curse, depending on the perspective. The names on the front side of the poster are these kinds of names.

The words and phrases on the back side of the poster are God's names for us. God sees us differently than the world sees us, than we see one another, or even than we see ourselves. God sees us for who we really are. We are awesome creatures. We are alive with a mysterious presence.

The Scriptures tell us that we are made from a mix of water and earth. Once we were formed, God breathed the breath of life into us. In Hebrew, the word *ruah* means "wind," "spirit," or "the breath of God."

During the process of Confirmation, you are invited to ask yourself an important question: What does God want of me? You are asked to make a choice and take a stand. When we celebrate the sacrament, you will be called forward by name to stand before the community. You will be anointed and sealed with the Holy Spirit, the Spirit of Jesus, *ruah* of God.

The seal of Confirmation marks Christians as people who choose to use their gifts and their freedom to live their life committed to the vision of Jesus Christ, that is, committed to love and serve others and to share the awesome gift of life as part of a community.

The choice is yours. You are free to stand by and watch, or you are free to participate in the life of the community and get involved in the life of other people as a disciple of Christ. During this retreat think about this question: Are you ready to make that choice?

Letter to God

1. Distribute to each participant a pen or pencil, and a copy of handout 1. Tell the young people to find a quiet spot where they can be alone with their thoughts and not distracted by other people. They are to spend the time quietly writing a letter to God.

When they are finished with their letter, they should not show it to anyone. Instead they should sign their name at the bottom of the letter, fold it, and give it to their small-group leader. Allow about 15 minutes for writing, though some people may need more time and some less.

2. When all the letters have been collected, call the young people back to the prayer space, put the letters near the candle, and thank the young people for their honesty and cooperation.

Choosing a New Name

Preparation. Write the following scriptural citations on newsprint. The phrases in parentheses are for your reference only.
◎ Ps. 139:14 (fearfully and wonderfully made)
◎ Gen. 1:27 (image of God)
◎ 2 Cor. 6:18 (son of God)
◎ 2 Cor. 6:18 (daughter of God)
◎ 1 Cor. 12:27 (Body of Christ)
◎ 2 Cor. 6:16 (temple of the living God)
◎ Isa. 44:1 (one of the chosen people of God)

1. Gather the young people in their small groups and distribute Bibles. Display the list of scriptural passages that you prepared before the retreat. Tell the young people that as a group, they are to find the name that God calls us in each passage. The small-group leader may want to assign a different passage to each group member. The names in the passages correspond to the phrase in parentheses next to each citation.

2. After the groups complete the task, tell the young people that you would like them each to pick a new name. Remind them of the importance of names, and caution them to think carefully before choosing a new name. When they choose a new name, they should write it on their name tag under their own name.

Encourage them to share their new name with the rest of the group and explain why they chose the name they did.

Close this part of the retreat by reading Isa. 43:1–5.

Recreation and Nutrition Break

Depending on your schedule, you may want to serve a meal during this break and give the young people an extended time for recreation. Consider scheduling small-group relay games, team-building activities, or other activities that will get the young teens working together.

Part 3: Relationships—the Water of Life (45 to 60 minutes)

Circles of Belonging

Preparation. Prepare a diagram of your own circles of belonging so that you can explain the concept to the participants.

Add a bowl of water and a branch to the prayer space.

1. Begin this activity by asking the following questions. Tell the young people that you do not expect them to answer the questions aloud. You just want them to think about their answers. However, you may want to solicit answers to the final question.

Have you ever felt out of place or alone?

When was the last time you felt like you really did not fit in?

Have you ever joined a group or tried to join a group?

Who are the people you belong with?

What is it that makes you feel like you belong?

2. Tell the group leaders to return the letters to God (from part 2 of the retreat) to their owners, along with a pen or pencil. The letters should be folded in half.

Explain to the teens the following process, displaying the model you created before the retreat:

Write the words, "Where I belong" at the top of one of the blank halves of the paper (on the back side of the letter).

Draw a small circle in the middle of the page. That circle represents you.

Draw concentric circles around the middle circle. You may use as many circles as you like, but start with three. In each circle write the names of the people and places that you belong to. The people you are closest to would be named in the circle nearest the center. Those who are just acquaintances would be named in the outermost circle. For example, the circle closest to you might include your mom and dad and your siblings. You belong with these people. You share a lot with them. The outermost circle might include a math class or your neighborhood. You belong in these places, but you do not necessarily feel a heart connection to these people.

In the end your circles will look like a pebble that has been thrown into the water. You are the pebble. The circles that form around you—your relationships—are like the waters of life. A person cannot survive physically without water. A person cannot live happily without being a pebble in the water that generates circles of relationships.

3. Allow about 10 minutes for the young people to complete their circles of belonging. Encourage them to do this exercise on their own and to fill in as many names as possible in each of the circles. You may want to set a minimum number for each circle, with larger numbers in the outer circles.

4. Allow about 10 minutes for the young people to share their circles with their small group. Pose the following questions as possibilities for discussion:

What is your closest relationship?

To what group do you feel like you most belong?

How many circles did you end up with?

How many circles included the parish or a faith community?

Did you include anyone in this room in your circles?

5. Make the following points in your own words, adding your own stories where it is appropriate to do so:

All people need to belong to someone or some group. It is easiest for us to belong when we share something in common, such as family, language, interest, friendship, or geography.

We all belong to the great circle of God. Our new names tell us where and to whom we really belong. We are all God's children.

We live inside lots of circles. We did not choose many of the people and communities we wrote down. We did not choose our family or the country we were born in. We did not choose our neighbors. But there are circles we choose to enter. Usually when a person chooses to join a formal group, a joining process or a ceremony occurs.

You are involved in a joining process right now. You are choosing whether to recommit to the church that someone else chose for you first. If you decide to recommit, you will confirm your choice when we celebrate the sacrament of Confirmation.

Baptism and the Eucharist are also sacraments of joining, or initiation, as they are officially called. But as a child, your understanding of what it meant to be a Christian was very limited. Now that you know more about who you are, you are ready for the next stage: the confirmation of your Baptism. It is time for you to state clearly and confidently where you really belong.

Remember that to belong to someone or to some group means to be able to give and receive. It is about working for a common goal. If you really belong, it means that you take on responsibilities and you make demands on the people you belong to. The more involved you are, the deeper your relationship will be.

Scriptural Puzzle

1. Give each small group a set of cards from resource 1. Announce that they are to put the cards in the order they think they belong in. The words on the cards are those of Jesus to his closest friends the night before he died, according to the writer of John's Gospel.

Allow about 5 minutes for the young people to work at the puzzle. When all the groups are finished, reveal the source as John 17:20–22, and tell them to check their results against the passage and rearrange their cards if necessary.

2. Invite the young people to recite the passage together. Explain that Jesus' prayer for his closest friends in the present and future—the people whose names he would write in the circle closest to his own—was a prayer that we would all be one. It was his invitation to be part of a bigger family. He is the pebble in the water. We are the circles around him.

3. Take the bowl of water from the prayer space. Once again, read the passage from John's Gospel. Dip the branch in the water and bless the participants, saying the following words as you do so:

May you remember the waters of your Baptism. May you be blessed with the waters of eternal life.

Recreation and Nutrition Break

Part 4: On Fire with the Spirit (60 to 120 minutes)

The Three C's

Preparation. Write your name on a sheet of newsprint. After your name, write the letters "CCC."

Write the following words on newsprint:

◎ caring	◎ critical	◎ called
◎ committed	◎ cool	◎ capable
◎ concerned	◎ challenged	◎ changing
◎ confident	◎ conscientious	◎ chaotic
◎ chosen	◎ careless	◎ cherished
◎ creative	◎ confused	◎ complete
◎ comfortable	◎ cornered	

1. Display the newsprint you created before the retreat with your name and the letters "CCC." Offer the following explanation in your own words:

Every baptized member of the community has three *C*'s at the end of his or her name. The *C*'s identify the person's denomination or particular branch of the faith tree (Catholic), his or her religious family (Christian), and the community he or she belongs to (church).

2.   Write the word "Catholic" at the top of a sheet of newsprint. Ask the young people to tell you what the word means. Write their ideas on the newsprint. Do the same for "Christian" and "church." Be sure the following characteristics are reflected:

Catholic. Universal; the wider church; a church with a long history and many traditions; a church that has much in common with other Christian churches; a church that differs from other churches in some forms of worship, the way it is organized, and in some key areas of belief

Christian. Followers of Jesus Christ who share a common Baptism and are committed to the Reign of God and to living out the law of love

Church. The people of God gathered together in worship; the people of God in service to others; the people of God making the Reign of God real in their midst

3.   Invite the young people to remove their name tag and write the letters "CCC" after their name, just as you had done. Point out that the three *C*'s are part of their qualifications for being confirmed. The letters are a sign of who they are, where they belong, and what they believe.

Announce that there is at least one more *C* that needs to be added. However, this time it is up to them to decide what it will be. Display the newsprint with the list of words. Tell the young people to look over the list, to choose at least one more *C* word that describes them right now in their faith journey, and to write that word or words on the back of their name tag. Encourage them to think through their choices and be able to explain why they chose at least one of the words. Their other choices can be kept secret. They should make their decision silently and not share it with anyone yet. After they finish writing, they are to put their name tag back on.

4.   Gather the young people into their small groups. Invite them to share at least one of the *C* words that they wrote on the back of their name tag and explain why they chose that word. Allow about 10 minutes for sharing.

5.   Close the exercise with a comment that the first three *C*'s—Catholic, Christian, church—define the community into which they are deciding whether to be confirmed. The *C* words they wrote on the back of their name tag define the nature of the flame of faith that they bring to the commitment.

Pentecost: The Beginning

Preparation. Decide which of the following three options you will use. Gather the appropriate supplies.

1. Explain that Pentecost is a very important day in the history of the church. See how much the young people know about the event by asking the following questions. If they do not know the answers, assure them that they will by the end of the activity.

What happened at Pentecost?

When did it happen?

Who was there?

Why is it an important day in the history of the church?

Option 1. Give each person a Bible and explain that Acts 1:12–14; 2:1–13 is the story of Pentecost. Announce that each small group should come up with a skit that portrays the event in a modern setting. Provide a variety of props and let the young people's creativity take over. Give them about 15 minutes to plan a skit, then have the groups perform for one another.

Option 2. Distribute a copy of handout 2 to each person. Divide the young people into two groups, facing each other. Lead them in an antiphonal reading of the story.

Option 3. Pass a Bible to each person. Form small groups and give each group a sheet of newsprint and some markers. Direct the small groups to rewrite on newsprint the story of Pentecost from Acts 1:12–14; 2:1–13, using modern imagery and language. They can be as creative as they want to be with the story. When all the groups are finished, ask them to read their stories to one another.

2. After the presentation of the story of Pentecost, ask the following questions:

Why would the title of this section of the retreat be "The Beginning"?

What happened at Pentecost?

When did it happen?

Who was there?

Why is it an important day in the history of the church?

What do the tongues of fire represent? the wind?

3. Present the following information in your own words:

Pentecost was a spiritually awesome experience that changed the life of everyone present. The two symbols the writer of Acts uses to describe this encounter with the Holy Spirit are wind and fire.

If you have ever seen or heard about a forest fire, you know that when wind and fire combine, they are capable of consuming everything in their path. The strong winds bring in oxygen to feed the flames.

The people who knew Jesus had just been through a major trauma. Often when people experience a tragedy, their first reaction is to withdraw, clam up, and be almost paralyzed with fear.

The Spirit of Jesus blew open the doors of people's lives. It charged them up and gave them a purpose. It set their spirits on fire. It was only when the Spirit came that the followers of Jesus could live up to who they really were.

Jesus promised his Spirit to all of us. The Spirit brings gifts to us so that we, too, can live up to who we really are. The Spirit changes us from "Lucy" to "Lucy, daughter of God, CCC" or from "Peter" to "Peter, carefully and wonderfully made, CCC."

When we celebrate the sacrament of Confirmation, all the people gathered are asked to pray for you, that your life will be transformed by this same Spirit that was present at Pentecost and at your Baptism. You need to be ready for this Spirit. You need to make space for the gifts being offered— if you choose to accept them.

4. End with the following questions, but do not solicit answers. Give the young people a few moments to think about their answers. Assure them that they will not have to share their thoughts.

Have you ever had an encounter with God that left you in awe?

Do you think the Pentecost story really happened as described in the Bible?

Are you ready to say yes to the Spirit?

Reflection: Gifts of the Spirit

1. Give everyone a copy of handout 3. Invite them to go somewhere in the room where they can be alone and fill out their prayer sheet. When they are finished, direct them to give the sheet to their small-group leader. Allow about 10 minutes for reflection.

2. When everyone is finished, conclude this part of the retreat by reminding them that the wind and fire of the Spirit on Pentecost spurred the disciples of Jesus to do great things for others and to serve the world in love. Our yes to the Spirit at Confirmation is a yes to making a difference in the world and to being dedicated to a life of justice.

Recreation and Nutrition Break

Part 5: What We Believe (45 to 60 minutes)

The Nicene Creed

1. Make the following comments in your own words:

On the day of Confirmation, you will be asked to stand up and state publicly what it is that you believe. This is something Catholics do every Sunday when they gather for liturgy. It is important that you know what the Catholic church believes.

Years after Pentecost, in A.D. 325, representatives from the many Christian communities gathered in the town of Nicaea and drafted a statement of faith. We call this the Nicene Creed. This creed—or statement of belief—is recited at every liturgy and has been affirmed by billions of people confirmed in the Christian faith over the years. The creed links us with Christians who lived more than sixteen hundred years ago and everyone in between.

2. Ask the young people to gather in their small groups. Give each small-group leader a copy of resource 2. Tell the young people that their leader will read the statements of belief slowly. At the end of each statement, they can ask questions and make comments. Assure them that it is okay to have questions about these beliefs. Then the leader will read the statement again. The participants who agree with the statement should say, "Amen" or "Yes!" or another word in affirmation. They should say it loudly and with conviction. The leader will then move on to the other sets of belief statements and follow the same process with each one.

Small-Group Exercise: We Also Believe . . .

1. Give each small group a sheet of poster board and some markers. Ask the young people if they see anything that could be added to the creed that applies to life in the twenty-first century. If they have trouble coming up with ideas, you might provide examples such as justice, hunger, respect, and the right to life.

Announce that as a group, they are to come up with two or three more belief statements that speak particularly to life right now and write them on the newsprint. Each statement should begin with the words, "We believe."

2. After the groups are finished with the task, invite them to share their additions with the large group. Note that they will use both the old creed and the new statements during the closing prayer.

Thank the young people for their cooperation and their willingness to explore some difficult faith issues.

Recreation and Nutrition Break

Part 6: Closing Prayer Service (30 to 45 minutes)

Preparation. Set up the prayer space with the candle, a Bible, the bowl of water and the branch used earlier, and four small bowls of bath oil or olive oil.

Recruit someone to read Isa. 11:1–2.

If possible, conduct this prayer service outdoors or in a room with many windows.

1. Gather the young people in a circle around the prayer table. Ask the small-group leaders to return their letters to God and their prayer for the gifts of the Spirit. They will also need the "We believe . . ." statements their group wrote during the creed exercise.

Make the following comments in your own words:

We have journeyed with the Risen Christ throughout this day. Our journey focused on the key elements of life: earth, water, air or wind, and fire. These are the basic elements of earthly life. They are also the basic elements of life as a follower of Christ:

Earth. We must be grounded in God, who is steady and always present.

Water. We must nurture and treasure our life-giving relationships with people and communities, those forged through the waters of Baptism and those formed through our hearts.

Air or wind. We must be open to the movement of the Spirit in our life.

Fire. We must invite and allow the Holy Spirit to fan the flame of our faith and set our heart on fire for justice and peace.

2. Ask the following questions and accept whatever answers the young people are willing to share:

What part of this retreat did you enjoy most? Why?

What was the most difficult part of the day for you? Why?

After they share their answers, announce that in this prayer service they are going to hand over the day to God and ask for the blessing of the Creator. Pray the following prayer or a spontaneous prayer on the same theme:

Creator God, we ask you to bless this circle of followers. We struggle to do justice, to walk in a humble way, and to be the servants of your Son, Jesus. Help us to live up to this calling, to stay grounded in you, to be open to the Spirit, and to listen as you call us by name. Amen.

3. Ask the volunteer to read Isa. 11:1–2. Pause for a few seconds after the reading, then invite the young people to read silently the prayer for the gifts of the Spirit that they worked on earlier. Encourage them to read aloud at least three times the gift that they underlined as well as the gift they requested at the bottom of the sheet.

4. Ask the young people to stand. Tell them you will read the Nicene Creed to all of them, just as their leader did earlier in the day. They are to respond loudly and enthusiastically, saying, "Amen!" or "Yes!" or whatever word of affirmation they used earlier. Read through each belief statement on resource 2 clearly and boldly, inviting the young people's response at the appropriate time.

Follow the statement of the creed with the "We Believe . . ." statements that each group wrote on poster board. Invite each group to read their statements aloud in unison so that everyone else can hear them clearly. After each group has finished reading the statements, ask the small-group leader to sprinkle them with water as a symbol of their Baptism.

5. Make the following comments in your own words:

Oil is a symbol of the healing power and presence of God. It is a necessary part of life. We eat it, cook with it, and cleanse, moisten, and heal our skin with it. It runs engines and is a source of heat and energy.

When leaders were chosen in ancient times, they were anointed with oil, just as you were anointed at Baptism as a child of God and a leader of God's people. During the celebration of Confirmation you will be anointed again, sealed with the Holy Spirit, as a sign of the commitment you are willing to make.

Ask the young people to extend both hands over the prayer space and the four bowls of oil. Say a prayer like the following:

Creator God, you have called us by name to be your children. You have blessed us with family, friends, and our community of faith. Bless this oil that will be a sign of our commitment to live the Christian way. We ask this in Jesus' name. Amen.

6. Ask the small-group leaders to come forward and take a bowl of oil back to their group. Explain the following process:

 Call each member by name, using also the name they chose earlier in the retreat. For example, "Sam Wilton, temple of the living God."

When the young person comes forward, everyone else in the group puts a hand on the person's shoulder, back, or head.

The leader dips his or her thumb in the oil and makes the sign of the cross on the person's head while saying, "Come, Lord Jesus, send _____ your Spirit. Renew the face of the earth."

Follow the same process for everyone in the small group.

7. Ask everyone to join hands. Thank them for their participation and cooperation. Close the retreat by reciting the Lord's Prayer together and sharing a sign of peace.

(This retreat was developed by Joe Grant, Archdiocese of Louisville, Kentucky.)

ALTERNATIVE APPROACHES

◎ The material in this retreat can get heavy at times for young teens as they explore issues of faith and the meaning of Confirmation. Consider extending the retreat day and adding time for games, simulations, and other opportunities to have fun and be creative. Consult another volume in the HELP series, *Community-Building Ideas for Ministry with Young Teens,* or other youth ministry resource books for ideas.

◎ To maintain a sense of solemnity throughout the retreat, use an alternative means of calling the group together instead of your voice. Consider using a bell, chimes, or a drum for this purpose.

For part 1: Getting started

◎ If the participants are at the upper end of the age bracket, you might have them introduce themselves to their small groups in the same way the leaders did. Have everyone state their name, which element they are more like, and why. Some younger teens, however, may not be at the intellectual stage where they can comfortably come up with an answer.

◉ As part of the group Scrabble game, assign points to each letter of the alphabet, just as they do in a real Scrabble game. Award prizes to the group whose words are worth the most points.

◉ If the group members do not know one another well and you have time, consider using additional icebreakers and mixers. For possibilities, check out another volume in the HELP series, *Community-Building Ideas for Ministry with Young Teens*.

◉ For the opening prayer, consider using Native American music for reflection. You might also teach the young people a simple Native American chant, such as "O Great Spirit." Recordings of such music can be found in larger music stores, through online sites, and in places that specialize in Native American resources.

For part 2: Wind, spirit, and the breath of God

◉ If the teens in your group are older, you may just want to hand out blank paper and have them write letters from scratch. Younger teens generally need a guided format, but once they reach age fourteen or so, they may benefit from having the freedom that a blank piece of paper allows.

◉ Set up oscillating fans around the room and have them blowing during all or part of this segment on the Spirit.

◉ To close part 2 of the retreat, conduct a naming ritual that highlights the themes of the session. For example, you might call each person forward, ask what his or her new name is, lay your hands on the person and say, "Ruah. With the breath of God, I call you _____ [new name]." It can be a simple ritual, but one that points out the significance and power of a name.

For part 3: Relationships—the water of life

◉ The concentric circle exercise can be done as a guided journal exercise. Lead the young people through a meditation in which they imagine and name all the people who are closest to them in their family, circle of friends, parish community, and so forth. Go through each circle this way.

For Part 4: On fire with the Spirit

◉ Consider doing the exercise in which the young people choose at least one more C word from the list as a journal exercise. Also, one-on-one sharing will provide for more intimate conversation if your young people are mature enough and willing to do it.

◉ If the young people have a good rapport with their small group, consider using the three questions that follow the presentation on the Spirit as a small-group discussion. You could also do it as a journal-writing exercise. Or, if you think they will be honest, do the exercise as a continuum exercise. Designate one end of the room as "yes" and the other side as "no." Explain that the young people are to place themselves on an imaginary line according to their level of certainty about each question.

◎ Depending on their catechetical experience, the participants may need a refresher on the seven gifts of the Spirit, the scriptural basis for the gifts, and what they mean in our life.

For part 5: What we believe

◎ As an exercise to see if the young people understand the faith statements in the Nicene Creed, divide the teens into pairs or groups of three. Give each pair or small group one sentence or small section of the creed and ask them to rewrite it in their own words.

For part 6: Closing prayer service

◎ If the young people are willing to sing, use appropriate hymns at various points in the prayer service.

◎ Instead of simply speaking the prayer while anointing with oil, the leader (or the whole group) can sing the blessing to an appropriate arrangement of the text, "Come, Lord Jesus, send out your Spirit. Renew the face of the earth." Replace the word out with the name of the person being anointed.

◎ Use the anointing with oil as an opportunity for affirmation. After the leader calls the person forward, he or she should invite others in the group to make positive comments about that person's gifts and strengths. The affirmation is followed by the signing with oil.

NOTES

Use the space below to jot notes and reminders for the next time you use this retreat.

Dear God

First, I'd like to thank you for . . .

Without these gifts, I would . . .

Some things I'm really struggling with right now are . . .

I wonder if you could help me . . .

Our leader asked us to think about if we are ready for Confirmation. On that topic, I'd like to tell you that . . .

Finally, God, I'd like to say that . . .

Love,

Handout 1: Permission to reproduce this handout for program use is granted.

Scriptural Puzzle

Make a copy of this resource for each small group. Cut the phrases apart as scored and mix them up.

I pray	**May they**
not only	**all**
for these,	**be one.**
my disciples,	**May they be**
but also for	**one in us,**
all those	**as you are**
who through	**in me**
their words	**and I am**
will believe	**in you.**
in me.	

(Adapted from John 17:20–22)

Resource 1: Permission to reproduce this resource for program use is granted.

79

The Beginning

A retelling of the story of Pentecost, from Acts of the Apostles 1:12–14 and 2:1–13. Form two groups, facing each other, and take turns reading.

Group 1. It was the feast of the harvest, fifty days after Passover, after the death and Resurrection of Jesus.

Group 2. The followers of the recently crucified Galilean were gathered together in an upstairs room in the capital city.

Group 1. These women and men, including Jesus' disciples and some of his relatives, were deep in prayer.

Group 2. Suddenly from the sky there came a great noise like the rush of a strong wind.

Group 1. The wind filled the entire house.

Group 2. With the wind came something that looked like fire, which settled above the heads of all those gathered.

Group 1. A holy and powerful Spirit entered the hearts of the entire assembly and prompted them to speak in many different languages.

Group 2. The city was busy with many pilgrims who came from different countries.

Group 1. Hearing the sounds of so many people speaking, a crowd of curious on-lookers gathered in the street.

Group 2. The bystanders were amazed and astonished at what they witnessed.

Group 1. Aren't these people Galileans?

Group 2. Then how come we can each hear them speaking and preaching about the wonders of God in our own language?

Group 1. There were some who tried to laugh it off. "They have been drinking too much new wine," they said.

Group 2. Peter, the leader of the followers, stood up and addressed the bystanders: "Listen, we are not drunk. It is only nine o'clock in the morning!"

Group 1. "On the contrary, what you are seeing and hearing is exactly what the prophet Joel foretold long ago."

Group 2. "In days to come . . . says our God . . . I will pour out my Spirit on all people; your sons and daughters shall prophesy, the old ones will dream dreams, the young people will see visions. . . . In those days I will pour out my Spirit. [adapted from Joel 2:28–29]

All. The beginning . . .

Handout 2: Permission to reproduce this handout for program use is granted.

Prayer for the Gifts of the Spirit

May the Spirit of God rest upon me.
May I be filled with the awesome and Holy Spirit of Jesus.

A Spirit of wisdom . . .
   to see myself and others with the eyes of God.
A Spirit of understanding . . .
   to see the heart of people and things.
A Spirit of counsel . . .
   to listen to the goodness within me and around me.
A Spirit of courage . . .
   to confront the dark and frightening things within me and the world around me.
A Spirit of knowledge . . .
   to know what is truly valuable in life.
A Spirit of holiness . . .
   to live a humble and prayerful life.
A Spirit of reverence . . .
   to walk, talk, and act in a way that is sacred and respectful.

Underline the one gift that you feel you need most in your life at this time. Is there another gift that you feel you need right now? If so, write it here:

_____

_____

Your Name _____

Our Statement of Belief

Do you believe in one God,
the Father, the Almighty,
maker of heaven and earth,
of all that is seen and unseen?
Response. **Amen.**

Do you believe in one Lord, Jesus Christ,
God's only Son,
eternally begotten of the Father,
true God from true God,
who, by the power of the Holy Spirit,
was born of the virgin Mary,
was crucified, died, and was buried.
Response. **Amen.**

Do you believe that on the third day
he rose from the dead,
ascended into heaven,
and is seated at the right hand of God?
Response. **Amen.**

Do you believe in the Holy Spirit, the giver of life,
who proceeds from the Father and the Son
and has spoken through the prophets?
Response. **Amen.**

Do you believe in the one, holy catholic and apostolic Church,
the resurrection of the dead,
and the life of the world to come?
Response. **Amen.**

This is our faith. This is the faith of the church.
We are proud to profess it in Christ Jesus our Lord.

(Adapted from the Nicene Creed, *The Rites of the Catholic Church,* volume 1
[New York: Pueblo Publishing Company, 1990], page 204, copyright © 1976,
1983, 1988, 1990 by Pueblo Publishing Company.)

Resource 2: Permission to reproduce this resource for program use is granted.

Following in the Footsteps of Jesus

A Retreat on Discipleship

OVERVIEW

This one-day retreat helps young teens grow in their understanding of the person of Jesus and explore what it means to be one of his young disciples, that is, someone who follows in his footsteps.

Suggested Time

This retreat can be done in 5 to 7 hours, depending on the size of the group and the length of the breaks.

Group Size

This retreat is most effective with groups of twenty or fewer. However, it can be done with any number of young people, divided into small groups, each led by an older teen or adult.

Materials Needed

- ☼ name tags, one for each participant
- ☼ pens or pencils
- ☼ a pillar candle and matches
- ☼ Bibles, one for the prayer area and one for each small group
- ☼ a variety of crosses and crucifixes

☼ newsprint and markers
☼ masking tape
☼ a small ball or other round object
☼ a tape or CD player, and a recording of high-energy music
☼ one hula hoop for every ten participants
☼ bags of M&M's, Skittles, or other multicolored candies, one bag for every six to nine participants
☼ a bowl
☼ a pair of dice for each small group
☼ two copies of resource 1, "Who Are You? Who Is Jesus?"
☼ copies of resource 2, "Report of a Missing Person," one for each small group
☼ 3-by-5-inch index cards, one for each person
☼ nine sheets of poster board, 22-by-28 inches each, plus one sheet for every two people
☼ a variety of used magazines and newspapers
☼ scissors, one for every two or three people
☼ glue sticks, one for every two or three people
☼ a ladder, a hammer, nails (optional)
☼ two similar objects, such as decorative pillows, shoes, or basketballs
☼ rope or cloth, two long pieces per small group
☼ remembrances of the retreat, such as a small cross or a copy of the prayer "Footprints" (optional)

PROCEDURE

Part 1: Gathering and Prayer (20 to 30 minutes)

Preparation. Make a sample name tag on newsprint, large enough for the entire group to see from a distance. Write your name in the center and one of the following sentence-starters in each corner:

◎ My favorite snack food is . . .
◎ My favorite soft drink is . . .
◎ My favorite Christmas story is . . .
◎ One thing Jesus taught is . . .

Set up a prayer space in the middle of the meeting room. Include in the space a pillar candle, a Bible, and a variety of crosses and crucifixes. Post the sample name tag on the wall in the prayer area.

1. Give each participant a name tag and a pen or pencil. Display the sample that you created before the session. Direct the teens to write their name in the center of the name tag and their answers to the sentence-starters in the corners.

2. Using an alphabetical list of the participants, pair the first person on the list with the last, the second person with the second to the last, and so forth, until all the teens have been assigned a partner. For example, Thomas Alvarez is paired with Joe Ziebell, Kristin Bennington is paired with Jaime Ybarra, and so forth. If you have an odd number of participants, assign a leader as a partner or create one group of three people.

Explain that the partners should introduce themselves to each other by sharing their name and their answers to the sentence-starters. Allow about 2 minutes for this task.

3. Gather the young people in a circle. Ask each person to introduce his or her partner to the rest of the group and share the information learned from the partner's name tag.

When the introductions are complete, you may want to give the teens an overview of the retreat day, especially if some of them have never been on a retreat. Answer their questions and find out what their expectations of the day are.

4. Invite the group to a moment of silence as you light the candle in the prayer space. Read the story of the call of the first disciples from Matt. 4:18–22. At the conclusion of the passage, continue the story by saying, "And Jesus continues to call disciples. Today he calls . . ." Divide the list of participants' names among the retreat leaders, and have each leader read the names on his or her list.

5. Conclude by reading the following prayer or a spontaneous prayer on the same theme:

O God, you sent your Son, Jesus, to lead people to goodness. As we begin this retreat, help us to be open to his call as we learn to be better disciples and followers of Jesus. We ask this in his name. Amen.

Part 2: Community-Building Activities (40 to 60 minutes)

Musical Antics

Preparation. Have available a tape or CD player, and a recording of high-energy music. Write the following list on newsprint and post it. Fold up the bottom to cover the list until it is needed. Note that you will be revealing only one action at a time.

Stand up and . . .
◎ crow like a rooster
◎ trade places with the person on your left
◎ turn around and yell your full name
◎ howl like a wolf
◎ trade places with the person three places to your right
◎ blow a kiss to the person on your right
◎ do an imitation of the wicked witch in *The Wizard of Oz,* sliding to the ground while saying, "I'm melting!"
◎ throw the ball in the air and catch it three times
◎ do two jumping jacks
◎ sing the alphabet song

While the young people are still in the circle from the opening prayer, give a small ball or another round object to one person. Explain the following directions in your own words:

When the music begins, the person with the ball passes it to his or her left. The ball continues around the group until the music stops.

Each time the music stops, I will reveal one action listed on the newsprint. The person holding the ball must perform that action. For the rest of the game, every time the music stops, everyone simultaneously stands up and performs the action he or she was assigned, and then sits down again.

When the music starts again, the person holding the ball passes it to his or her left. When it stops, I will reveal another action. The process continues until all actions are revealed.

Hula Hoop Game

Divide the participants equally into small groups of about ten people. Have each small group form a circle with their hands joined. Direct two people to separate their hands. Place a hula hoop between them and ask them to rejoin their hands. Explain the following directions in your own words:

The object of this activity is to move the hula hoop around the circle until it returns to the place where it started.

The players may not let go of their partners' hands. They must step through the hula hoop and get it over their body with their hands joined.

The first group to get the hula hoop completely around the circle wins the game.

All About Me

Preparation. Decide how many young people will be in each small group. Place an equal number of each color of M&M's, Skittles, or other multicolored candies in a bowl, so that the total number of candies equals the total number of participants.

1. Pass the bowl of candy around the group and direct the young people to each take one piece of their favorite color. Before they eat the candy, tell them to gather with those who chose the same color of candy that they did.

2. Give each small group a bag of M&M's or other multicolored candies. Tell the participants to take as many candies as they want, but not more than they can hold with one hand. Be sure that everyone in the group gets some candy.

3. Announce that everyone must tell the group one thing about themselves for each candy that they took. If someone took four candies, that person must share four things about himself or herself. If another person in the group took twenty candies, that person must share twenty facts. Direct each of the groups to select a leader. The participants will remain in the same small groups throughout the retreat.

Seven-Eleven

Preparation. Write the following list of questions on a sheet of newsprint and post it. Include the numbers.

2. What is something you are proud of having done with a friend?
3. Where do you want to visit in your lifetime, and who do you want to travel with?
4. What is the best thing a friend ever gave you?
5. What is a controversial issue among you and your friends?
6. Who is one friend you admire? Why?
7. What would you and your friends do to change the world—if you could do it and not fail?
8. You win a bonus pick! Choose and answer any question between one and twelve, except eleven.
9. What is one thing a friend influenced you to change your mind about?
10. What is one thing you have experienced that you hope your friends never have to go through?
11. You win a bonus pick! Choose and answer any question between two and twelve, except seven.
12. What is one thing you would change at school for the sake of your friends?

Give each small group a pair of dice. Explain that each person, in turn, should roll the dice and answer the question on the newsprint that corresponds to it. Go around the group as many times as the schedule allows.

Recreation and Nutrition Break

Part 3: Who Is Jesus? (60 to 75 minutes)

The Missing Jesus

Preparation. Recruit two volunteers to read resource 1.

1. Direct the young people to reconvene in their small groups. Introduce this section by making the following comments in your own words:

If you want to know about someone, check out the person's friends. People choose friends with whom they are comfortable. The friends you choose reveal something about you.

The same is true for Jesus. If you think about all the different types of people Jesus was friends with, it says a lot about who he was. Our task is to discover some of the qualities of Jesus and be able to answer the question Who is he?

2. Ask the two volunteers that you recruited before the retreat to read aloud the reflection on resource 1. After the reading allow a few moments for silent reflection.

3. Give a copy of resource 2 to each small-group leader. The form contains the same type of information that would be found on a police report for a missing person. Tell the participants to pretend their friend Jesus is missing. They want to find him. To do so, they must work together in small groups to complete the report. Allow about 20 minutes for each group to complete the report.

4. Call the groups together, and give each small group a chance to share and explain its answers. Clarify any misinformation before moving directly into the next segment on friendship with Jesus.

I Call You Friends

Preparation. Recruit someone to read John 15:11–17. Write the following questions on newsprint:

◎ What do you most like to do with your best friend?
◎ If Jesus came to your home today and asked if he could be your friend, what would you most look forward to doing with him?
◎ In what ways can you live and act like a friend of Jesus?

Create a large crucifix by taping together five sheets of 22-by-28-inch poster board lengthwise. Tape two more sheets onto each side to form a cross. Ask someone to lie down on the cross with arms outstretched, like the body of Jesus. Trace that person's body. At the top of the cross, write "Embracing." At the bottom, write "Friendship."

Gather a variety of used magazines and newspapers.

1. Invite the person you recruited before the session to read John 15:11–17. Explain that Jesus' invitation to friendship was meant for all who believe in him, that is, all who are willing to be his friend.

2. Give each person an index card and a pen or pencil. Display the newsprint list of questions that you prepared before the retreat, and invite the young people to spend a few minutes writing answers to the questions on their index card. Allow about 5 minutes for writing.

When time is up, ask the young people to gather with their small group and share their answers to the questions. While the young people are in their small groups, lay the poster-board cross in the middle of the meeting space.

3. Gather the young people around the cross and distribute a marker to each person. Invite them to write their name inside the corpus on the cross. Make the following points in your own words:

Jesus opened his arms to embrace people in friendship, to embrace all of life. Many people in our world do not feel Jesus' embrace. They are in pain, lonely, scared, angry, or convinced that they have no friends, not even Jesus.

Distribute a variety of magazines and newspapers, scissors, and glue sticks to the participants. Ask them to find pictures, stories, and headlines that represent people or areas that need the embrace of friendship. They might also find pictures that illustrate an embrace. All the pictures and news stories should be glued inside the corpus, being careful not to obscure the participants' names. Encourage them to fill the corpus with pictures and stories.

4. Ask the young people to clean up the work area. Reverently move the cross to the prayer space. Lay it on the floor, or, if possible, post it on a wall. It may take many hands, a ladder, and a hammer and nails to accomplish this goal. When the cross is moved, invite the young people to kneel around it for a moment of silent prayer for all those people who need to feel the warmth of Jesus and the embrace of his friendship.

Recreation and Nutrition Break

Part 4: Working Together (50 to 65 minutes)

1. Tell everyone to take off their shoes and pile them in the center of the room. Ask the following questions, soliciting a variety of answers from a number of different people:

Do you like your feet? Why or why not?

Are your feet ticklish?

Describe your favorite pair of shoes.

When was the last time you walked barefoot?

When was the last time someone washed your feet for you?

2. Direct the young people to find the same partner they had for the opening of the retreat. Point out the pile of shoes, and explain that each partner should explain what his or her shoes look like to the other. Each person must find his or her partner's shoes simply based on description. No one can provide any directions other than a description of the shoes themselves.

3. Direct the young people to stand in two parallel lines, facing their partner. When everyone is in line, divide the parallel lines in half to form two teams. Explain the following process in your own words and then begin the activity:

Extend your right hand and take the left hand of your partner. Everyone's hands should be crossed in front of them.

Sit down with your partner so that your legs are outstretched, but in a way that you can bend your elbows if you need to.

I will put an object [pillow, shoe, or basketball] on the crossed hands of the first pair on each team. The object of the game is to use only your interlocked arms and hands to move the object down the line and then back again. You may not toss the object over several pairs.

The first team to get the object to the other end and back wins the game.

4. Tell the young people to gather with their small group and stand in a single-file line. Using rope or long strips of cloth, tie their legs together at the knees and the ankles. Assign each group a route of about the same distance. If possible, include challenges like an incline or winding hallways.

Announce that the task of each small group is to move from one point to the other with their legs tied to one another. Give them time to come up with a strategy. Emphasize that this is not a competition.

5. When all groups have accomplished their task, ask the following questions:

What made each of the following tasks difficult?

finding your partner's shoes

passing the object down the line and back

moving in small groups with your legs tied together

What made you successful?

What do these games have to do with being a friend of Jesus in and to the world?

Recreation and Nutrition Break

Part 5: Following in the Footsteps of Jesus (60 to 70 minutes)

Small-Group Performances

1. Distribute at least one Bible to each group, and assign each group one of the following scriptural passages:
- Matt. 22:36–39
- Matt. 25:31–40
- Mark 10:17–25
- Luke 18:15–16
- John 13:3–15
- John 15:1–5

Explain that the small groups have about 40 minutes to figure out a creative way to get the message of their passage across. They can do a skit, a song, a rap, a commercial, and so forth. The only rule is that everyone in the group must be involved in some way.

2. When the groups are ready, invite them to perform their creations for one another. Affirm their creativity and reiterate the message of Jesus that is part of each passage.

Closing Prayer

Preparation. Cut a footprint for each person out of poster board. The footprint should be three to four times the size of an adult foot.

1. Gather the young people in the prayer space. Light the candle. Give each person a marker and one of the footsteps you created before the session. Invite them to consider what they will do to show the world that they are a friend and disciple of Jesus. They are to write their action on their footstep. Allow about 5 minutes for the young people to complete the task.

2. Read aloud Col. 3:12–17. Then call each young person by name and ask her or him to read the action written on her or his footprint. After each person shares, invite the group to respond, "Clothe yourself with Christ." When all are done sharing, ask the participants to place their footprint at the foot of the cross that you created earlier in the session.

Thank the young people for their participation in the retreat. Challenge them to continue to live as if Jesus is their best friend. You may want to give each person a small remembrance of the retreat, such as a small cross or a copy of the prayer "Footprints."

(This retreat was developed by Carole Goodwin, Archdiocese of Louisville, Kentucky.)

ALTERNATIVE APPROACHES

For part 1: Gathering and prayer
◎ For other ideas for creating pairs, check out another volume in the HELP series, *Community-Building Ideas for Ministry with Young Teens.*

For part 2: Community-building activities
◎ If your group is large, you may want to add a few more actions to the list for the first circle game. If your group is very large, you may want to break it into two circles and conduct simultaneous games.
◎ The hula hoop game also works well as a noncompetitive activity. Simply eliminate the last direction.
◎ If you prefer to assign the participants to small groups, eliminate the first step of the M&M activity.

For part 3: Who is Jesus?
◎ To make a more permanent cross, use 1-by-6-inch boards. Eliminate the corpus. After the young people glue pictures, headlines, and news stories, apply a thin coat of shellac to hold everything in place. Keep the cross as a permanent reminder of the embrace and the sacrifice of Jesus.
◎ If you have an instant camera, take a photograph of each person and add the photos to the corpus of Jesus on the cross.

For part 4: Working together

◎ If you want to expand this session, another manual in the HELP series, *Community-Building Ideas for Ministry with Young Teens,* contains a variety of team simulation games.

For part 5: Following in the footsteps of Jesus

◎ Consider using a messy but meaningful alternative to the footprint cutouts. Cover the bottom of a disposable aluminum roaster pan or cookie sheet with poster paint. Direct the young people to remove one shoe and sock, step into the poster paint, and add their footprint around the edge of the cross. Provide a number of pails of soapy water and towels for quick cleanup.

Make a number of permanent markers available. After the paint has dried, have the young people write on their footprint the gifts and talents they possess.

◎ If your group is small, personalize the reading from Colossians in the closing prayer by inserting the names of the participants at the opening and closing of phrases.

NOTES

Use the space below to jot notes and reminders for the next time you use this retreat.

Who Are You?
Who Is Jesus?

Reader 1. My friends are popular and known by everyone.

Reader 2. I was born an unknown to a peasant family.

Reader 1. I love to visit my friends' homes and see all the stuff they have.

Reader 2. When I was born, my family was homeless and had nothing.

Reader 1. My friends are above average and in the smart group at school.

Reader 2. I grew up in a small rural town. I did not go to school. I worked as an apprentice in a carpenter's shop.

Reader 1. My friends are all planning to go to college and get degrees.

Reader 2. I learned how to read, but I never learned how to write. I never earned a degree.

Reader 1. My friends are planning to have successful careers and make lots of money.

Reader 2. When I left home and my family, I became a vagrant who depended on handouts to survive.

Reader 1. My friends and I plan to travel all over the world.

Reader 2. I never went further than one hundred miles from where I was born.

Reader 1. My friends are expecting to be someone important someday. They are very loyal to one another.

Reader 2. I never had any money, and I never had prestige among the people in my hometown. My friends did not stick up for one another. No one wanted to be around them, but I loved them!

Resource 1: Permission to reproduce this resource for program use is granted.

Report of a Missing Person

Full name of missing person _____

Aliases _____

_____

Last known address _____

Other known addresses _____

_____

Age _____ occupation _____

Employer _____

Previous occupations _____

Special skills _____

Last seen _____ date _____ time _____

Location _____ by whom? _____

Describe clothing person was wearing when he was last seen _____

_____

_____

Physical Description _____

_____

Height _____ Weight _____ Color of hair _____

Color of eyes _____ Ethnicity _____

Distinctive physical characteristics (scars, tattoos, handicaps, and so forth) _____

_____

_____

Name and occupation of all known acquaintances _____

_____

_____

_____

_____

Other pertinent information _____

_____

_____

_____

_____

By His Cross and Resurrection

A Retreat on Triduum Themes

This retreat is designed as a one-day experience, but it can also be used as an overnight event. The retreat plan includes creative, active, and reflective activities and stories from the Scriptures to recall the Passion, death, and Resurrection of Jesus.

Suggested Time

This retreat will take between 4½ and 6 hours with breaks. It can be extended to an overnight experience by using some of the alternative approaches.

Group Size

This retreat is most effective with groups of twenty or fewer. However, it can be done with any number of young people, divided into small groups, each led by an older teen or adult.

Special Considerations

This retreat is best used on the day of the Easter Vigil, or at least during the period of the Triduum. However, it can be effective at any time during the season of Lent. Also, because of the serious, reflective nature of the event, it will be most effective with young teens at the higher end of the age range, such as seventh and eighth graders.

Materials Needed

- stick-on name tags, one for each person
- construction paper (optional)
- glue sticks, at least one for every two people
- a hole punch (optional)
- a ball of yarn (optional)
- an instant camera and film (optional)
- index cards, one for each person (optional)
- two or three hula hoops
- front panels from cereal boxes, one for every six to eight people
- a scissors
- a paper bag
- cellophane tape, one roll for every five to six people
- newsprint and markers
- masking tape
- a large piece of butcher paper, cardboard, or cloth
- a crucifix (not a cross), preferably the parish's processional crucifix
- a Bible
- seven votive candles and matches
- a tape or CD player, and a recording of reflective music (optional)
- a pitcher of warm water and a basin
- several towels
- a loaf of bread on a plate
- a pitcher of grape juice
- a chalice or a large clear glass
- a purifier or another small cloth for wiping the chalice rim
- a variety of used news magazines and newspapers
- scissors, at least one for every two people
- masking tape
- pieces of $1/2$-inch wide ribbon in a variety of lengths, 24 to 36 inches each, four pieces per person
- the parish's paschal candle or a large pillar candle
- a bowl of water
- a small container of olive oil or bath oil
- a taper candle or wick

PROCEDURE

Part 1: Getting Started (30 to 60 minutes)

1. As the young people arrive, give each person a stick-on name tag. Or if you have an extended period of time, you might ask them to be a little creative with their name tags. Two options follow here:

◎ Each person tears the letters of her or his first name out of construction paper. The letters are glued together with the edges slightly overlapping. Punch a hole or two in the letters and attach a piece of yarn so that the name tag can be worn around the neck.

◎ When the young people arrive, take a picture of each of them with an instant camera. Have them attach their picture to an index card and write on it their name and the phrases, "Child of God, disciple of Christ." Invite them to decorate their name tag creatively. Punch one or two holes in the top and string enough yarn through so that the tag can be worn around the neck.

2. Lead the young people in some simple mixers, icebreakers, and get-to-know you activities so that they feel comfortable with one another. Use the suggestions below, or consult the volume in the HELP series entitled *Community-Building Ideas for Ministry with Young Teens,* which contains several strategies for bond building.

Pass the Hula Hoop

Direct the teens to stand in a circle and link hands with the people on either side of them. Separate one pair of hands and re-link them through the opening of a hula hoop. Announce that the object of the game is to pass the hula hoop around the circle without letting go of anyone's hands. They must figure out a way to get each person through the hoop without breaking the chain of hands.

When the hoop has been passed around the circle, start again. This time add a second hula hoop and perhaps even a third, starting each hoop at a different point in the circle.

Cereal Box Puzzles

Preparation. Cut the front panels from boxes of breakfast cereal into puzzle pieces. The number of puzzle pieces for each panel depends on the number of people you want to have in each small group. Six to eight people in a group is best. Put all the pieces for the panels in a bag and mix them up.

While the young people are still in the circle from the hula hoop game, distribute the puzzle pieces. When everyone has a piece, announce that they are to find the people whose puzzle piece is from the same cereal box. When they find one another, they must sit down and tape the cereal box panel back together. Provide each group with a roll of cellophane tape.

Things in Common

1. Give each small group a sheet of newsprint and some markers. Designate one person as the recorder, using an objective way of choosing a leader. For example, you might designate the person with the most letters in her or his first and last names, or the person whose house number adds up to the biggest total.

Explain that as a group, they are to find ten things that everyone has in common. The recorder's task is to write the ten ideas down. Obvious facts are not allowed, such as, "We're all human" or "We all have ten fingers" or "We're all in junior high." Tell them to try to find out a little more about one another through this exercise. Give them examples such as these:

◎ Everyone was born in a different state.
◎ Everyone has at least two grandparents who live nearby.
◎ Everyone plays a team sport.
◎ Everyone has played a musical instrument.
◎ Everyone has read all the Harry Potter books.

2. When the groups are finished, ask them to share their results with everyone. Post the lists in an obvious place so that the teens can read about other groups during their break.

Part 2: Introduction and Prayer (45 to 60 minutes)

Preparation. Recruit three people to each read a Scripture passage, and give them a chance to look over the readings.

Mark the following passages in the Bible:

◎ Mark 15:21–26
◎ Mark 15:27–32
◎ Mark 15:33–37

Make a life-size cross out of butcher paper, cardboard, or cloth. Cut the cross into puzzle pieces equal to the number of participants.

1. Review the lists of things group members have in common, and see if any characteristics or experiences are common to all the lists. Start a new sheet of newsprint, and ask the teens to name things that everyone in the room has in common. If they are stumped, direct them to faith-related items, such as the following:

Everyone was created by God.

God loves each person and knows each person through and through.

Through his death and Resurrection, Jesus redeemed us and all of humanity.

We are all called to follow Jesus and be like him.

List as many items as you have room for on one sheet of newsprint. Post the sheet with the other lists. Explain that during this retreat, they will explore together what all Christians have in common: a belief that the Passion, death, and Resurrection of Jesus is the foundation of their faith. For two thousand years, people who have called themselves Christian have celebrated these events in the life of Jesus. The church continues to do so in the twenty-first century.

2. Ask the teens to reflect quietly on that thought for a few seconds. While they are doing so, create a prayer space in front of the group with a crucifix (preferably a processional crucifix), a Bible, and three votive candles at the base of the crucifix. If possible, dim the overhead lights.

Ask the first volunteer to read Mark 15:21–26 and then light the first votive candle. After a moment of silence, ask the second reader to read Mark 15:27–32 and then light the second candle. Again, after a few moments of silence, ask the third person to read Mark 15:33–37 and light the last candle.

Invite the participants to close their eyes and reflect silently on the death of Jesus and the reactions of the people around him. This reflection should last for about 3 minutes. If you have a recording of quiet instrumental music, play it at this time.

3. Close this time by offering the following prayer or a spontaneous prayer on the same theme:

O Jesus, when you died your mother and friends gathered at the foot of the cross and wondered why. We gather at the foot of this cross and wonder why. But you promised that your death would not be the end. We look forward to Easter, the fulfillment of your promise. And in your name we pray. Amen.

4. If you have dimmed the lights, bring them up at this time. Leave the candles lit. Give each person a marker and one of the puzzle pieces from the cross you made before the retreat. Ask the young people to think about someone they know who is like Jesus. It could be a parent, a friend, a relative, an acquaintance, or someone they have heard about. Tell them to write that person's name on their puzzle piece along with a short phrase that describes why that person reminds them of Jesus. Do not tell them that the pieces form a cross.

5. Distribute rolls of cellophane tape and announce to the teens that they must now assemble the puzzle, but do not tell them that the finished product will be a cross.

After the cross is assembled, invite the participants to offer their ideas about why the pieces formed a cross rather than another symbol. After listening to their thoughts, ask them to place a hand on the cross on or near their puzzle piece. When everyone is settled, read the following prayer:

May we always be blessed with people in our life who remind us that all of us are supposed to do what Jesus did in his life, like _____ [read the names and comments on the puzzle pieces, or invite the young people to read their choices]. We thank you, God, for the gift that these people are to us and to the whole world. Amen.

Recreation and Nutrition Break

During this break put the cross off to the side but in a place where it will be visible by everyone for the rest of the retreat.

Part 3: The Last Supper (about 30 minutes)

Preparation. Recruit two volunteers to each read a Scripture passage. Mark the following passages in the Bible:
◎ Matt. 26:26–30
◎ John 13:1–15

Recruit one or more adults to have their feet washed in case no young people volunteer.

Add two votive candles at the foot of the crucifix (leave these unlit while the others remain lit), a pitcher of warm water, a basin, several towels, a loaf of bread on a plate, a pitcher of grape juice, and a chalice or large clear glass.

1. Gather the young people in front of the prayer space that you used in part 2. Request that they focus silently on the crucifix and recall the incidents from Jesus' last days that the candles represent.

Ask the first volunteer to read Matt. 26:26–30 and then light a candle. After a moment ask the second volunteer to read John 13:1–15 and follow the same procedure.

2. If the young people are not already seated in chairs, set some chairs in front of the group. Call for volunteers to have their feet washed, and have them sit in front of the group. If no young people volunteer, call on the adult(s) that you recruited before the retreat.

Remind the participants that this was a powerful prayer moment for the followers of Jesus. Peter did not want Jesus to wash his feet, but when Jesus told him that this would show how good a follower he was, Peter agreed. Request that the young people observe the washing silently.

Using the pitcher and the basin, wash the feet of those who have volunteered. Do both the washing and drying slowly and prayerfully. If you are using reflective music, you might play it at this time. Then wash and dry the hands of all the other people in the room. If you have a large group, you may want to have other adults help with this task so that you can move through the entire group in a short amount of time. However, be sure to maintain an atmosphere of reverence.

3. Ask the young people the following question:

In what ways do people in the community give their bodies—their strength, time, or talent—to serve others?

Invite them to share their answers. Some obvious examples include doctors, teachers, ministers in the church, and homeless-shelter workers.

Call one young person to come forward and hold up the plate containing the loaf of bread. Remind the group that Jesus shared bread with his followers and told them that it was his body to be broken for them. Just as Jesus did, many people in our world give totally of themselves to make the world a better place. We are all called to do the same.

Invite the teens to share specific names of people they know who give their all for others. Then take the plate from the person who is holding it, and tell her or him to take a piece of bread and eat it. Return the plate and ask the holder to serve the next person. Continue passing the bread until everyone has gotten a piece.

4. Invite one of the young people to hold up the pitcher of grape juice. Ask the following question and invite the young people's responses:

Who in our community puts their life on the line for others?

Some examples are a police officer, a firefighter, a soldier, and so forth.

Remind the teens that when Jesus shared the cup he said that it was his blood, which was poured out for us. Invite the teens to share specific names of people they know who put their life on the line for others. Then pour the juice into the chalice or glass and offer it to the person who was holding the pitcher. Wipe the cup, then follow the same procedure as you did with the bread to distribute the juice to the rest of the group.

You may want to give the young people a stretch break before moving into part 4. Leave the candles lit for the next activity.

Part 4: The Garden and the Cross (60 to 75 minutes)

Preparation. Add two unlit votive candles to the prayer space. Recruit two more volunteers to read the Scriptures. Mark the following passages in the Bible:
◎ Mark 14:32–46
◎ Luke 23:35–46

Write the following questions on newsprint:
1. Where and how in your school or community do people experience fear; emotional, spiritual, or physical violence; or unjust treatment?
2. Where in the world do people experience violence, horror, mistreatment, injustice, fear, and prejudice?
3. Who is doing good things for those who suffer injustices at your school? in the community? in the world?
4. How is God's presence made known, even amid evil?

1. Invite the first volunteer to read Mark 14:32–46 and then light a votive candle, as in previous sections. Allow a few seconds of silent reflection before moving on.

2. Tell the young people to move into the same small groups that they were in at the beginning of the retreat. Give each small group a sheet of newsprint, a variety of magazines and newspapers, scissors, and glue sticks.

Display the questions you wrote on newsprint before the retreat. Tell the small groups that they are to discuss the four questions for a few minutes. Then they are to find pictures, words, and stories that represent the answers to the first two questions and use them to create a collage on one side of the newsprint. On the other side, they are to create a collage of pictures, words, and stories that answer questions three and four.

As the groups finish their task, post the collages with the answers to the first two questions facing out. If possible, post the collages so that they are visible from the prayer space.

3. Gather the participants in the prayer space. Invite them to a moment of silence while they look at the examples of violence, horror, mistreatment, injustice, fear, and prejudice. After about 30 seconds, tell the young people to continue looking at the posters while the second volunteer reads Luke 23:35–46 and then lights a candle.

4. Ask the teens to close their eyes. Explain that you will read four situations, and you would like them to think about times when they found themselves in the same situation. Read the following statements, pausing about 30 seconds in between each to give the participants a chance to reflect:

Remember a time when you were rejected or rejected someone else.

Remember a time someone made fun of you or you made fun of someone else.

Remember a time when you were angry, mean, or when you lied or cheated.

Remember a time when you were forgiven.

Give each person four pieces of ribbon and a marker. Have them write on each of the ribbons their experience of one of the four situations. Emphasize that this is to be done silently and privately. You may want to suggest that they move to a part of the room where they can be alone with their thoughts. Tell them that the ribbons will be tied to the crucifix, but no one will get a chance to read what's on them.

As they finish their ribbons, have the young people tie them to the processional crucifix.

Part 5: Resurrection Celebration (45 to 60 minutes)

Preparation. Recruit a volunteer to read Luke 24:1–12. Mark the passage in the Bible.

1. If possible, do this final segment in the church around the paschal candle. If it is not possible to use the church, set up the parish's paschal candle or a large pillar candle in another part of the retreat space from where the rest of the activities have taken place.

Have someone carrying the crucifix with all the ribbons streaming from it lead the group to the area where the paschal candle stands. Also have all the people who read the Scriptures carry their lit votive candles in procession. The person who volunteered to read the passage from Luke should carry the Bible. Ask someone from each small group to carry the collage poster they created with the representation of the answers to the final questions facing out. Also have someone else carry a bowl of water and a small container of oil. Gather everyone around the paschal candle. If possible, put the posters up on a wall near the candle. If not, lay them on the floor.

2. Remind the teens that one of the most common symbols of Easter is a large candle, which represents the passage from death and darkness to life and light. The paschal candle is blessed at the Easter Vigil at every Catholic church in the world and is lit during sacramental celebrations at the parish.

Ask the last volunteer to read aloud Luke 24:1–12 and then use a taper candle or a wick to light the paschal candle. Direct all those who have votive candles to extinguish them.

3. Place the bowl of water and the oil near the paschal candle. Direct everyone to extend their hands in blessing over the water. Say the following prayer or a spontaneous one on the same theme:

Come, Holy Spirit, bless this water and oil and make them holy. It is a reminder to us of our Baptism, when we became children of God. May we also become Easter people who have chosen to follow the way of Jesus. We ask this in his name. Amen.

4. Invite the group members to come to the bowl one at a time and bless themselves with the water as a reminder of their Baptism. Then pass the oil around the group. Have each person anoint her or his neighbor by tracing the sign of the cross on her or his forehead and stating, "Remember, _____ [name], you are a child of the Resurrection. Go now and show others the Spirit of the Risen Christ."

5. If it is appropriate to do so, conclude with an Easter party or celebration of some sort.

(This retreat was developed by Joe Grant, Archdiocese of Louisville, Kentucky.)

ALTERNATIVE APPROACHES

◎ This retreat would work well as a parent-teen activity.
◎ Consider breaking this retreat into five sessions and doing one session weekly during the season of Lent. Conclude the series by attending the Easter Vigil together.
◎ If you want to extend this retreat to an overnight experience, you may want to show a movie like *Godspell; Jesus Christ Superstar; Jesus of Nazareth;* or another film version of the life, Passion, death, and Resurrection of Jesus.

For part 2: Introduction and prayer
◎ Instead of brainstorming in the large group, challenge the small groups to come up with a list of ten faith-based characteristics they have in common. This exercise will take more time than doing it as a large group.
◎ If you have a large group, you may want to give each smaller group pieces from one section of the cross. Tell them to take their pieces and assemble their section of the cross. Then bring the sections together and assemble the entire cross. As you are doing so, comment on the universality of the church and how we are all united by the cross of Jesus.
◎ Assemble the cross by gluing the pieces to a sheet of plywood to make a lasting reminder of the retreat and its message.

For part 3: The Last Supper

◉ If you have a large group, use several plates and cups. Break the loaf of bread evenly among the plates and pour the juice into other cups. Start them at different points in the group.

◉ To add more movement to this part of the retreat, allow each person to add to their puzzle piece at the appropriate time the names of people who give their all and people who put their life on the line.

For part 4: The garden and the cross

◉ Intensify the garden experience by inviting adult leaders, young adults, or high school leaders to share their stories in response to the following "remember" questions.

   I remember a time when . . .

   ◉ I was rejected or rejected someone else.
   ◉ someone made fun of me or I made fun of someone else.
   ◉ I was angry, mean, or lied or cheated.
   ◉ I was forgiven.

This adds a witness talk or faith story dimension to the retreat, and younger adolescents are particularly interested in the faith stories of older youth or adults.

◉ The collage activity will undoubtedly lighten the atmosphere, provide movement, and add noise to what has been a somber hour. If you would rather maintain the quiet, reflective mood, consider one of these options:

   ◉ Just have the adult leader conduct a discussion based on the questions.
   ◉ Have each person silently make his or her own collage on a sheet of notebook paper. Play reflective music during this time.
   ◉ Post four sheets of newsprint or butcher paper. Ask the teens to silently look through the magazines and newspapers and find a story, word, or picture that answers each of the questions.

◉ If possible, hang the collages suspended from the ceiling so that both sides are visible.

◉ To avoid confusion, you may want to write the four "Remember a time . . ." statements on newsprint. If you choose to do this, do not display the newsprint until you distribute the ribbons.

For part 5: Resurrection celebration

◉ Time the retreat so that the group can join the parish celebration of the Easter Vigil. If you choose this option, omit part 5.

◉ Consider leading the young people in a simple chant while they are processing to the candle. Many of the chants from Taizé are short, simple to sing, and do not take a lot of rehearsal. The music and recordings are available through GIA Publications, 7404 S. Mason Avenue, Chicago, IL 60638-9927, phone 800-442-1358.

- If the church or school has grounds (woods, a garden, or a lawn), enhance the experience by quietly moving the group outside, processing with candles or flashlights, and gathering around the processional cross.
- If you have extra time, consider doing this last part outside. Give everyone a small piece of paper and a balloon. Tell them to write words and phrases that are associated with Easter, such as *Alleluia! He is risen! Rejoice!* or *This is the day the Lord has made!* Put the paper inside a balloon, fill the balloon with helium, and tie it off. When the reader gets to Luke 24:5, "He is not here, but has risen," signal the teens to release their balloons so that they carry the good news of the Resurrection.
- You may want to provide taper candles with drip protectors to each person. As people come up to be anointed with water and oil, have them light their taper from the paschal candle.
- Continue the retreat with a service project by doing an Easter-egg hunt for local children, singing Easter songs and delivering daffodils to shut-ins, or volunteering to serve a meal at a soup kitchen.

NOTES

Use the space below to jot notes and reminders for the next time you use this retreat.

Let's Get Rolling

A Leadership Day for Young Teens

This retreat introduces young teens to basic leadership skills, such as making decisions based on values, solving problems cooperatively, accommodating and celebrating personal differences, and planning balanced programs based on the components of total youth ministry.

Suggested Time

The total time for this retreat is estimated at 6 hours. However, you can easily expand the retreat to 8 hours by extending activities and discussions, adding alternative approaches, and providing more recreation and nutrition breaks.

Group Size

This retreat is most effective with groups of twenty or fewer. However, it can be done with any number of young people, divided into small groups, each led by an older teen or adult.

Materials Needed

- plastic name badges with inserts, one for each person, or a button machine with button parts

- a variety of used magazines and newspapers
- scissors, one for each person
- glue sticks, one for each person
- a box, bag, or bowl
- newsprint and markers
- one copy on card stock of resource 1, "Table Roles," for every four or five participants, cut apart as scored
- one copy on card stock of resource 2, "Who's At the Table?" for every four or five participants, cut apart as scored
- one copy of resource 3, "Clues for 'Who's At the Table?'" for every four or five participants, cut apart as scored and folded
- a plastic cup or envelope, one for every four or five participants
- scrap paper, one sheet for every four or five participants
- pens or pencils
- one copy of resource 4, "'Who's At the Table?' Solution," for every four or five participants
- one die for every twenty people
- blank paper, one sheet for each person
- masking tape
- a box of assorted chocolates, large enough so that each person gets one piece
- four sheets of poster board
- four Bibles
- a candle and matches
- one copy of resource 5, "Prayer Cards," cut apart as scored
- a basket
- one copy of resource 6, "Taskmaster's Guide," for every four or five participants
- one copy of handout 1, "Commercial Skit Ideas," for each person
- a strip of crepe paper at least 20 feet long
- one party balloon plus a few extras
- a coin
- a bell
- a Bible
- a ball
- a plastic or ceramic fish
- a globe
- a key
- a bandage
- a cross
- one copy of resource 7, "Youth Programming Ideas," cut apart as scored
- cellophane tape or glue

PROCEDURE

Part 1: Getting Started (about 35 to 50 minutes)

Preparation. Place used magazines and newspapers, scissors, glue sticks, and colored markers in the craft area.

1. As the young people arrive, give each one a plastic name badge with a blank insert. Escort them to the craft area and direct them to create a mini-collage that represents who they are. They are to do this by cutting out small pictures and words from magazines and newspapers and gluing them to the insert. After the entire insert is covered, they are to cut out the letters of their name and glue them over the collage. The letters should be large enough to be read at a distance.

2. When everyone has had a chance to complete a name tag, collect all the name tags and put them in a bag, bowl, or box. Randomly pull out groups of four or five name tags and call out the names. These people will form a small group. Tell them to find a space and sit down together.

When everyone has been assigned to a small group, direct the participants to figure out who in the group has a birthday closest to today. That person should stand. When one person from each group is standing, tell the young people that they will take turns explaining their name tag to the other group members. Direct the people who are standing to sit down, and announce that the person to the right of the person who was standing should explain her or his name tag first. Proceed around the group, ending with the person who stood at the beginning of the activity. Allow about 1 minute for each person in the group to share.

3. Write the word *leader* at the top of a sheet of newsprint. Ask the young people to call out words and phrases that come to mind when they hear the word. Fill the newsprint with their ideas. When the sheet is full, explain the purpose of the retreat by putting the following ideas in your own words:

Everyone possesses the necessary tools to be an effective leader. These are the same tools you use in daily life: communication, cooperation, problem solving, planning, and getting things done.

Everyone is a leader is some way. If you play on a team, baby-sit, have younger siblings, or do group projects at school, chances are that you have exercised some leadership skills, whether you knew it or not.

The purpose of this retreat is to use the tools you already possess and develop them in a way that will allow you to effectively lead others in your school or parish. You will learn how to work together to plan activities that will help everyone in the group grow personally, spiritually, and communally as Christians.

4. If necessary, give the young people a stretch break before moving on to the next section.

Part 2: Cooperating (60 to 90 minutes)

Who's At the Table?

1. Put a set of cards from resource 1 facedown in the middle of each small group. Use all five cards for groups of five. Eliminate one of the two praisegiver cards for groups of four. Tell the young people not to touch the cards until told to do so.

When you have distributed the sets of cards, announce that each person in the group must take a role card from the pile and look at it. He or she is to act the role on the card throughout the activity.

Ask the taskmasters to raise their hands. Describe and demonstrate the role they are supposed to play in the activity. Do the same for each of the other roles until you are sure that everyone knows what they are supposed to be doing.

3. Place in the middle of each group a set of cards from resource 2, a set of clues from resource 3 folded and placed in a plastic cup or an envelope, a pen or pencil, and a sheet of scrap paper. Explain the following directions in your own words:

Create an imaginary dinner table in the center of each group. Separate the four directional signs from the other cards and put them in their proper place around the table: starting at the top and moving in a clockwise direction, the signs should read north, east, south, and west. These directional signs outline the dinner table for a fictional family.

The groups' task is to place the "Who's At the Table?" cards in their proper location at the table, using the clues they have. They have 15 minutes to accomplish the task. Everyone is to maintain their assigned role throughout the activity. When they have finished the task, they will have the answers to the following questions.

Who is seated in which place at the table?

What is the age of each child at the table?

What is the occupation of each adult at the table?

What is each person's dinner preference?

4. Do not warn the participants when the end of their time is drawing near. Leave that job to the person who drew the taskmaster role in each group. After 15 minutes, call time. Usually one group will finish ahead of time and yell out,

"We did it! We did it! Look at what we did! Is it right? Did we do it right?" In this case go over to the table and look at their solution. If it is correct, tell them it's perfect. If it isn't correct, give them clues such as, "Look again at this part" or "You have one part wrong." If everyone isn't finished when time is called, give each group leader a copy of resource 4 and go over the answers together. That way the group members can cheer for the ones they got right, add on the ones they didn't have, or just switch around the ones they had wrong.

5. Gather the young people in the center of the room and engage them in a discussion around the following questions:

What did you like or dislike about your role?

How was your role important in the group?

What did you like or dislike about the process? Was it fun? frustrating? too easy?

Was your group successful? Why or why not?

How is this challenge like challenges at school or at home?

How is it different?

What did this exercise have to do with being a leader?

Emphasize that you did not have them do this exercise to learn how to arrange people at a table. You wanted them to learn about working together as a group with a taskmaster, a gatekeeper, a praisegiver, and a notetaker, so that they could see how all these roles are important. Mention that you will be talking about these roles for the rest of the day and practicing them in other ways.

Dice Game

Preparation. Write the following list on newsprint.
Tell about a time when you felt . . .
1. proud
2. angry
3. sad
4. afraid
5. excited
6. tired

1. Preface this activity by noting that one of a leader's most important tasks is to listen to other people and to get to know who they really are. One way to get to know other people is to listen to their stories.

2. If your group consists of twenty or fewer people, do this exercise as one large group. If you have more than twenty people, break into two groups. Throw out a numbered die. Display the newsprint list of topics you created before the session. Explain that they are to roll the die and, based on the number they roll, tell a story that corresponds to that number on the newsprint list.

Allow the storytelling to go on until time runs out. Affirm the young teens for their willingness to tell their own stories and to listen to the stories of others.

Label Making

1. Gather the participants into one group. Recruit volunteers to be label makers. Give each volunteer several sheets of blank paper and a marker. Ask the other participants to call out labels that are often applied to people at school. Some examples might be jock, nerd, geek, skater, cool, popular, and so forth. When a participant calls out a label, direct one of the volunteers to write the word on a sheet of paper. Continue the process until the volunteers have created one label for each person in the group. If the teens run out of ideas before enough labels are created, duplicate some of those already created.

2. Tape a label on the front of each person. Try not to give anyone a label that might duplicate how their peers really see them. For example, give a girl who is generally considered to be popular a label that she is not used to wearing. Give a boy who is considered by his peers to be a geek a label that allows him to step outside of that role.

Announce to the participants that they will have 2 minutes to move around the room, acting and treating other people in a way that is suggested by the label they are wearing. Encourage them to talk to as many people as they can.

3. Call time and gather the participants together. Lead a discussion around the following questions:

How did people treat you because of your label?

How did you treat others because of their label?

How did it feel to be treated according to your label and to treat others that way?

Why is it important for a true leader to look beyond labels?

4. Pass around a box of assorted chocolates. Tell the teens to take one piece of candy, but to try to guess what's inside before they bite into it. When everyone has taken a piece, close the activity by pointing out that one thing that stands in the way of people really getting to know one another is the labels we give other people. When we treat people according to artificial labels, we lose the opportunity to find out who they really are and what their gifts may be. Paraphrase the famous line from the movie *Forrest Gump,* "Life—and people—are like a box of chocolates; you never know what you're going to get."

Recreation and Nutrition Break

Part 3: Taking a Stand (45 to 60 minutes)

Memory Check
To help the teens focus on the next part of the retreat, engage them in a discussion of what has happened to this point in the day. Use these or similar questions:

What have we done so far?

What did these activities have to do with leadership?

How can what we have learned help us in life?

Write their answers on newsprint and post them in a visible place in the room. Add to the list throughout the day so that at the end of the retreat, the participants can see at a glance everything they learned about leadership and about life.

Where Do You Stand?

Preparation. On paper or poster board, make the following signs. Post the signs in the four corners of the room.
◎ I strongly agree.
◎ I think I agree.
◎ I think I disagree.
◎ I strongly disagree.

1. Gather the teens in the middle of the room. Explain the following directions in your own words:

I will read a statement. You are to move to the corner that best represents your opinion about the statement. Anyone can move to a different corner at any point, as long as the corner you move to more fully expresses your opinion on the issue.

I will ask different people to explain and justify their opinion. I will play devil's advocate by disagreeing with whatever they say, and they must continue to explain their position and try to convince me that I am wrong.

Anyone in any corner can express an opinion at any time. This activity is not intended to be a discussion between the leader and one or two people.

The comments must focus on the issues and should not be demeaning or personal.

2. Present as many of the following statements as time and energy allow. Use those that you think will create interest and a diversity of opinion in your group. Feel free to add your own statements based on current events in the community.

There is too much violence on television.

People who are rich should be required to give money to those who are poor.

A woman should be the president of the United States.

Parents should make their children go to church with them.

The mother in a family has it harder than the father.

You can't make it in life without a college degree.

People who waste natural resources or don't recycle should be fined.

Teenagers eat too much junk food, don't get enough exercise, and generally are not concerned about their health.

Professional athletes make too much money. All they do is play a game, so they should not make more money than teachers, who train the leaders of tomorrow.

The true test of success is how rich a person is.

Life gets easier the older a person gets.

If the government lowered the drinking age, teenagers would drink responsibly.

3. Review and process the exercise by leading a discussion around the following questions:

What was it like to have to defend your opinion against someone who you knew would disagree?

How did it feel to have everyone watching you as you spoke?

What did you learn about your feelings toward others who disagree with you on important issues?

How does it feel when someone you really like disagrees with you?

Did any opinions or comments surprise you?

What did your opinions on the issues tell you about yourself?

Thank the young people for expressing their honest opinions, and affirm them for trying hard to articulate their thoughts. Point out that knowing what they believe and being able to articulate and defend their opinions are essential qualities and skills of a good leader.

Jesus Questions

Preparation. Recruit four readers. Assign each reader one of the following passages:

- Mark 10:13–16
- Luke 19:1–9
- Mark 5:25–34
- John 8:1–11

1. Gather the young people in the center of the room. Pose the following questions and see how they respond. You may want to write their answers on newsprint.

What would you do if you were going for a walk with your friends and your little brother or sister wanted to tag along?

What would you do if your classmates were making fun of you for hanging around with unpopular people?

What would you do if you had something that someone else wanted, but instead of asking you, they just took it?

What would you do if some bullies were ganging up on one person and wanted you to join in?

2. Pose the following version of each question again, and ask the teens what they think Jesus would do. Assure them that Jesus did, in fact, find himself in each situation, and see if they can identify a story from the Gospels that applies. After each discussion tell the Gospel story briefly, then ask the volunteer you recruited before the session to read the corresponding scriptural passage.

When was Jesus with his friends when children showed up? What do you think he did?

Although the Apostles scolded people for bringing their children and bothering Jesus, he told the children to come to him so he could hold them and bless them. [Mark 10:13–16]

When did people make fun of Jesus for hanging around with unpopular people? What do you think he did?

Jesus ignored their comments. He told Zacchaeus, a hated tax collector, that he would like to have supper with him that night. Later Zacchaeus decided to pay back the money he took from people. [Luke 19:1–9]

When did someone want something from Jesus, but just took it instead of asking? What do you think he did?

A woman wanted Jesus to heal her. Instead of asking him, she just touched his cloak. She was cured immediately. When Jesus realized what had happened, he did not scold her. Instead he complimented her on her faith. [Mark 5:25–34]

When did a bunch of bullies try to pull Jesus into ganging up on somebody? What do you think he did?

A group of Pharisees brought to Jesus a woman who was accused of adultery, claiming that she should be stoned according to the Law. Jesus told them that the person who had no sins should be the first to throw a stone at the woman. Eventually all the Pharisees left. Jesus forgave the woman. [John 8:1–11]

3. Summarize the activity by stating that we can and should try to imitate Jesus with our actions. We could be more welcoming to people who are unpopular or younger than us. We could defend people who are being attacked or wrongly criticized.

Prayer Cards

Preparation. Set up a prayer space in the middle of the group. Place the prayer cards from resource 5 in a basket.

1. Gather the young people in a circle around the prayer space. Light the candle. Tell them that you will pass around a basket of cards with prayer intentions on them. Each person should choose a card, read the description, and then say a short prayer for that person. Caution them not to name particular people when doing so might hurt the person, for example, "someone you dislike" or "an unpopular student at school."

2. When all the cards have been distributed, pass the empty basket around the group and collect the cards in it. Put the basket back in the prayer space and close with a short, spontaneous prayer asking for God's blessings and help.

Recreation and Nutrition Break

Part 4: Making a Difference (about 75 minutes)

Memory Check

As you did at the beginning of part 3, engage the teens in a discussion of what has happened to this point in the day. Use these or similar questions as they apply to the group's work on "Taking a Stand."

What have we done so far?

What did these activities have to do with leadership?

How can what we have learned help us in life?

Commercial Skits

Preparation. Write the following topics on newsprint. Add other topics that are appropriate for your group or in your community.
◎ Using alcohol, tobacco, and other drugs is a big mistake.
◎ We need to take care of the earth so that it can take care of us.
◎ Helping the poor is everyone's responsibility.
◎ Violence is wrong.
◎ Staying in school and getting good grades is important.
◎ It's good to go to church, and we're proud to be Catholic.

1. Divide the participants into small groups. They may work in the same groups that they were in for earlier activities, or you may want to create new groups. Designate someone to take on each of the roles assumed in the "Who's At the Table?" activity:
◎ taskmaster
◎ gatekeeper
◎ praisegiver
◎ notetaker

You can just designate specific people for roles, such as "the oldest person in each group is the notetaker." Or you can follow the same process that you did in part 1. Once again tell the teens that they are to maintain their assigned role throughout the activity.

2. Announce that each small group will select a topic and create a 30-second commercial to sell its point of view. Display the newsprint list of topics you created earlier. Give the participants about 2 minutes to talk with other group members and decide which topic they will choose from the list.

While they are deciding, give each group a sheet of newsprint and a marker and a copy of resource 6. Give each person a sheet of scrap paper and a pen or pencil and a copy of handout 1.

3. Explain that the taskmaster in the group has the instructions for creating the commercial skit. Turn the process over to the taskmaster and let the events unfold. After 25 minutes invite the groups to perform their commercial skits for one another.

4. Close the activity by affirming everyone's creativity, cooperation, willingness to listen to other people's ideas, and ability to work together toward a common goal. Point out that each of those qualities is essential in leadership and in life.

Crazy Volleyball

1. Divide the young people into two groups. Designate one group as the "Praise the Lord" group, the other as the "Alleluia" group. Set up a "net" in between the two groups by stringing crepe paper between two walls or objects. The crepe paper should be at least 4 feet off the ground.

Blow up a balloon and insert a coin in it before tying it off. Be sure that the balloon is made of sturdy latex like that used in party balloons.

2. Announce that the group will play a game of crazy volleyball. Explain the following rules in your own words:

The object of the game is much like regular volleyball. That is, each side must hit the balloon over the net and keep it from hitting the ground on their side of the net.

When either side wins a point, they are to shout together, "Praise the Lord" or "Alleluia," depending on the name they were given before the game started.

After each point, everyone must rotate positions. The rotation must involve at least one player on each side moving to the other side of the net.

3. Toss the balloon into play and observe the game. Do not offer clarifications or explanations of the rules. If they choose to change the rules, offer no objections.

4. After about 5 minutes of play, gather the group and lead a short discussion around the following questions:

Who won?

How did you feel about not having definite teams?

Why did you (or didn't you) change the rules?

What did this game have to do with leadership? with life?

If the young people played the game without becoming competitive, congratulate them and affirm that the best leaders are not competitive. Rather, they try to get everyone working together. If they changed the rules to make the game more competitive, explore the pluses and minuses.

5. Close the activity by talking about the importance of cooperation and of having fun together without winners or losers. Competition certainly plays an important role in life, but much more is accomplished through cooperation. The good of all is ultimately more important than the glory of a few.

Finding Our Place

Preparation. Set on a table in the middle of the meeting space the following items:

- a bell
- a Bible
- a ball
- a plastic or ceramic fish
- a globe
- a key
- a bandage
- a cross
- a basket with the slips of paper from resource 7

Write each of the following words or phrases at the top of a separate sheet of newsprint or poster board. Draw a picture of the corresponding item.

- advocacy (bell)
- catechesis (Bible)
- community life (ball)
- evangelization (fish)
- justice and service (globe)
- leadership development (key)
- pastoral care (bandage)
- prayer and worship (cross)

1. Briefly explain the concept of youth ministry to the young people as a response of the church to the needs of young people and an invitation to young people to share their gifts with the larger community. Youth ministry has eight elements, symbolized by the eight items that are on the table in the middle of the group. Tell the teens that you will describe each element briefly.

As you describe the components, hold up the corresponding newsprint. As you finish each description, invite one person to tape the newsprint to the wall. Use your own words to make these descriptions come alive for your group, but keep them short.

Advocacy (bell). We ring a bell so that people hear it. Sometimes no one hears the voices of young people. Advocacy means that we want to be sure that young people's voices ring out loudly and strongly, so that adults know what young people think, feel, and need. An advocate is someone who speaks on behalf of another person so that his or her needs are not forgotten.

Catechesis (Bible). Young people do not always know all about the Catholic faith. Sometimes they have questions about the Bible, they want to know who Jesus really is, or they wonder why we celebrate sacraments like Baptism or the Eucharist. When young people learn about what the church says and does, what Catholics believe, and how they live out their faith, we call that catechesis.

Community life (ball). The Catholic church around the world is one community, with the Holy Spirit acting within each believer. Each parish is a special community. We become part of community life when we get to know one another and start to care about one another. Anytime we do something to improve our relationships with one another, we improve our community life. Sometimes that means playing games or sharing stories. Sometimes that means just being there when someone is sad.

Evangelization (fish). When people are serious about being followers of Jesus, it affects their whole life. Jesus called his followers to be fishers of people. Evangelization means that everything we do and say encourages others to be more faithful and to live the way Jesus taught us.

Justice and service (globe). The church calls its members to be peacemakers and to defend the rights of those who are not being treated with dignity. We serve the needs of the poor, the homeless, and the hungry all over the planet. When we do these things, we are working for justice.

Leadership development (key). Everyone has something to offer. Everyone has something to learn. Keys unlock doors of opportunity. Leadership development happens when young people are trained to better use their talents and gifts to serve others.

Pastoral care (bandage). Young people face a lot of difficult decisions as they grow up. Pastoral care is the support and guidance they receive from loving adults who listen to them. Sometimes young people have deep hurts and wounds that need to heal. Sometimes pastoral care involves connecting young people with the resources needed to help them make choices that are physically and spiritually healthy.

Prayer and worship (cross). God is always communicating with us. When we become aware of God's presence and respond to it, that is prayer. Because young people are hungry for God, it is important to provide them with many ways to pray and to experience the presence of God.

2. Divide the participants into eight groups. Give each group one of the symbols. One by one, take the programming ideas from the basket and talk about where they belong. Many of the ideas apply to more than one component. Engage the young people in a discussion about where each fits best. Give the paper to the group that is holding that symbol.

When all the slips of paper have been distributed, provide tape or glue and have the young people attach the slips to the appropriate newsprint. Then invite the teens to look over the lists and add to them any other ideas that they can think of.

3. Give each person a pencil, pen, or marker. Invite everyone to write their initials next to the two or three ideas that sound most appealing to them under each component. Emphasize that by placing their initials next to an activity, they are not committing to doing it, but simply indicating interest.

When everyone has had a chance to add her or his initials to each sheet, look at all the components and determine which activities seem to command the most interest. Assure the young people that you will follow up. If you are not in a position to make things happen, tell them that you will pass along the information to the people at their parish or school who have the authority to do so.

Part 5: Let's Get Rolling (about 20 minutes)

1. Gather the young people in a circle. Review the "memory check" sheets that you posted throughout the day. You may want to add another sheet listing the learnings from part 4 of the retreat, "Making a Difference." Spend a few minutes discussing the same questions that you posed earlier in the day:

What have we done so far?

What did these activities have to do with leadership?

How can what we have learned help us in life?

2. Retrieve the ball that you used in part 4. Explain that though the day was full of fun and learning, it is only a beginning. It is time now to get the ball rolling and use what they learned on the retreat to strengthen their personal relationships and contribute to the good of the church and the world.

Tell them that you will roll the ball. Whoever touches the ball should say a short prayer about the day, their hope for their parish or school, or anything else they want to pray for. When they finish, they are to roll the ball to someone else. Continue until time is up or until everyone has had a chance to express their thoughts.

Thank the teens for their participation, energy, attention, and enthusiasm.

(This retreat was developed by Lisa-Marie Calderone-Stewart, Archdiocese of Milwaukee, Wisconsin.)

ALTERNATIVE APPROACHES

For part 1: Getting started

◎ If the group members do not know one another, you may want to start with one or two mixers or icebreakers. Consult the volume in the HELP series entitled *Community-Building Ideas for Ministry with Young Teens* or a similar resource. You will need to add extra time to the schedule if you choose to conduct additional activities.

◎ Instead of the collage name tags, make a connection to Catholic Tradition by having the young people make a name tag about their patron saint. Saints are, after all, leaders in our faith tradition. Make available a variety of books on saints and baby names. Have the young people look up the meaning of their name and write it on their name tag underneath their name. Then have them read about their patron saint and write words on their name tag that describe that person. If their name has no connection to a saint, have them read about the saint whose feast day is the same day as their birthday.

For part 2: Cooperating

◎ You can save time by preparing a box for each group with all the necessary materials for the activity. Put each set of cards or clues in a separate envelope.

◎ Instead of having the groups recreate the table on the floor, give each group a sheet of newsprint and a few glue sticks. Have them tape the cards to the newsprint, then post the results of their work toward the solution.

◎ To give the young people a chance to get to know their peers, you may want to form new groups for the dice game and again for the label-making activity. One option is to collect all the name tags and form random groups the way you did at the beginning of the retreat. You will also find many more ideas for creating groups in *Community-Building Ideas for Ministry with Young Teens,* another volume in the HELP series.

- If you have time, close this section of the retreat with a short prayer service during which the young people take each other's labels off, tear them, and put the pieces in a pile to be tossed in the trash. Use an appropriate prayer about seeing beyond the surface of a person from *Looking Past the Sky: Prayers by Young Teens* or *Life Can Be a Wild Ride: More Prayers by Young Teens,* both published by Saint Mary's Press.

For part 4: Making a difference

- Instead of having each group do a skit from the list that is provided, have them come up with their own ideas. You may want to take 5 or 10 minutes to do some brainstorming with the full group before they begin work in small groups.
- If you have a large group, make the crazy volleyball game more interesting by putting more than one balloon in play. Try playing with one or even two balloons on each side of the net.
- If you have time and are in a position of youth leadership, spend some time with the young people prioritizing the activities and making initial plans. Doing so will keep their enthusiasm high and give them a reason to come back.

For part 5: Let's get rolling

- You may want to provide each person with a memento of the retreat. For example, you could give each person a card with the components of youth ministry and a prayer for young people, a painted rock, or a religious symbol.
- Consider expanding the prayer into a commissioning service for the newly trained youth leaders.

NOTES

Use the space below to jot notes and reminders for the next time you use this retreat.

Table Roles

Make a photocopy of this resource for each small group of four or five people. Cut apart the roles as scored. You may want to fold each paper so that no one can read the role but the person who picks it.

Taskmaster

Ensure that the group sticks to the task and keeps on the time schedule.

Gatekeeper

Ensure that everyone has a chance to talk and everyone listens.

Praisegiver

Ensure that everyone gets complimented and that the group stays positive.

Praisegiver

Ensure that everyone gets complimented and that the group stays positive.

Notetaker

Keep track of what is said and write it down.

Who's At the Table?

Make a photocopy of this resource on card stock for each small group of four or five people. Cut apart the sections as scored.

north	south	east	west
adult	vegetarian
seven years old	Chris
Justin	bookstore clerk
pancakes, French toast, and waffles	does not like fish or seafood
Pat	Sherry
Brenda	Nathan
adult	ten years old
cheese soup	salad with dressing on the side
sixteen years old	steak, sausage, and pork chops
artist	thirteen years old

Clues for "Who's At the Table?"

Make a photocopy of this resource for each small group. Cut apart the clues and fold them in half and then in half again. You may want to put the clues for each group in a plastic cup or envelope.

Four children and two adults live together in this family.	The ten-year-old sits across the table from the sixteen-year-old.
One of the adults works at a bookstore and does not like fish or seafood.	Nathan sits across the table from Pat.
Justin likes his salad with the dressing on the side.	Sherry sits between her parents.
Nathan sits between his ten-year-old brother and his seven-year-old sister.	One of the parents sits across the table from the girl who likes to eat French toast, pancakes, and waffles.
Chris and Pat love their four children.	The thirteen-year-old loves to eat sausage, steak, and pork chops.
The seven-year-old sits next to the artist.	One of the adults sits on the east side of the table.
The ten-year-old sits next to the person who does not like seafood or fish.	Every time this family sits down together to eat, they sit in the same seats.
Chris works at a bookstore.	Brenda is seven years old.
The boys in the family are ages ten and thirteen.	The sixteen-year-old is a vegetarian.
The girls in the family are ages seven and sixteen.	Pat is an artist who loves cheese soup.
The vegetarian sits between the artist and the bookstore worker.	Brenda sits at the west side of the table.
Sherry and Pat sit on the south side of the table.	Justin sits next to his thirteen-year-old brother.

"Who's At the Table?"
Solution

North

```
        Nathan, age thirteen              Justin, age ten
        sausage, steak, and               salad with dressing
        pork chops                        on the side


West    Brenda, age seven                          Chris, adult       East
        waffles, pancakes,                  no fish or seafood
        and French toast                      bookstore clerk


            Pat, adult                         Sherry,
            cheese soup                       age sixteen
            artist                            vegetarian
```

South

Resource 4: Permission to reproduce this resource for program use is granted.

Prayer Cards

Make a copy of this resource on card stock and cut the petitions as scored. Place them in a basket, bag, or box. You could also make a copy on plain paper, cut the intentions apart, and glue or tape them to index cards. If your group is small, choose the petitions that seem most appropriate. If it is larger than the number of petitions, duplicate some of them. Feel free to add other intentions that may be particular to your community.

A teenage boy who is not good at sports and hates himself	The president of the United States
A poor Mexican farmworker who does not speak English and needs a job	A teenage girl who does not have any friends because people make fun of her clothes
A teenager who hates going to school because of the racial prejudice he experiences there	A woman in China whose husband and sons have been kidnapped
A teenager who is trying to decide whether to drink alcohol with his friends the next time they ask	The bishop of this diocese
Your best friend	A teenage girl who was raped by her brother's friend and is afraid to tell anyone
A teenager who does not get along with her mother	A teenage girl who is pregnant and scared
A runaway teenager who has not had a meal in three days	Your favorite teacher
A teenager whose father left her mother when she was a baby	An older Native American who hates his life because his tribe and culture are dying off

A family whose father just got killed
in a drive-by shooting

A young adult who just found out that
her HIV test came back positive

A young adult
who cannot find a job

A teenager who is trying to make good decisions,
but is hanging around with friends who do drugs

Someone
you dislike

People from Cuba who are trying to make their
way on an overcrowded boat to a better life in
the United States, but are denied entrance

Someone you had a fight with
this week or this month

A teenager who hates
going to church

A family that
is homeless

A teenager who
has cancer

A teenager whose mother died
when he was a child

A starving child
in Africa

A teenage boy who
believes that he might be gay

An unpopular student
at your school

A teenager who does not get along
with his father

Someone
from your family

A person
in this room

A teenager whose older brother
committed suicide

Taskmaster's Guide

As the taskmaster of the group, your job is to see to it that the participants follow this process:

1. Everyone thinks of one idea and writes it down. This should be done silently. (4 minutes)

2. Each person shares his or her idea with the group. The notetaker writes everyone's idea on a sheet of newsprint. (4 minutes)

3. Each person talks about his or her new favorite idea and the group members plan what they will do. The commercial should be about 30 seconds long, and everyone in the group should have a speaking part. (4 minutes)

4. Practice the commercial skit. (12 minutes)

5. Show time!

Commercial Skit Ideas

Here are some ideas for putting together a commercial skit to sell your group's point of view. Let your imagination wander. One of these ideas may spark a new one for you. You do not have to use an idea on this list if you come up with something else.

- A famous person tells his or her opinion and explains it.

- Someone states the opposite opinion. Others tell him or her why that opinion is wrong.

- Everyone tries to convince the viewers with a good reason for their opinion.

- Group members act out a story showing how something good happened because of the right choice.

- Group members act out a story showing how something bad happened because of a wrong choice.

- Group members write new words to a well-known song or jingle to express their opinion about the topic.

Youth Programming Ideas

Make a copy of this resource and cut it apart as scored.
Feel free to add your own ideas to this list.

A regular meeting at which young people can talk about their problems or anything else they want to discuss	A workshop on parent-teen communication
Young people invite senior citizens to a "senior prom," a party and dance just for them	A workshop on teen depression and how to cope
An overnight camping trip	Visiting people who are confined to their home or to nursing facilities
A canoe trip	CROP walk, to raise money for hungry people
Help decorate the church for different liturgical seasons	An afternoon of writing letters to political leaders about important issues
A card-writing night to people in college, the military, prison, and so forth	Gospel plays or stations of the cross done by teens
Leadership skills workshops for youth and adults	A planned fast to raise money for the poor
A peer ministry team, where young people are trained to help other youth who are having problems	Events that raise money for victims of natural disasters
A workshop on how to deal with conflict	Opportunities to learn about the Catholic faith
Support groups for teens with special concerns, such as divorce, death, addictions, and so forth	A core planning team made up of youth and adults

An outreach event for young people who do not attend church	Helping with a kindergarten religious education class
A monthly breakfast discussion of the Sunday readings	An overnight retreat
Religious education classes	A workshop on materialism at a local mall
A Bible study group	Making sandwiches for homeless people
A youth bulletin board at church	Collecting school supplies for children in a poor area
A fun event shared with youth from a non-Catholic church	A night of movies and box games
Listening sessions between the youth of the church and the pastor	A bike-a-thon
A youth newsletter	A trip to a concert by a Christian artist
A thank-you meal for parents, cooked and served by young people	A trip to a diocesan or national youth rally
A prayer journey	A meeting with the parish pastoral council to discuss youth concerns
Young people sharing the homily with the priest at Mass	Baking cookies with scriptural verses in them for a local soup kitchen
Performing music and skits for nursing home residents	Picking up trash in honor of Earth Day

Appendix 1

Connections to the Discovering Program by HELP Strategy

"Let Your Light Shine: An Overnight Retreat on Self-Esteem"

As presented, this retreat complements the following Discovering courses:

◎ *Becoming Friends*
◎ *Making Decisions*
◎ *Understanding Myself*

"Beneath Our Masks: An Overnight Retreat on Being True to Oneself"

As presented, this retreat complements the following Discovering courses:

◎ *Becoming Friends*
◎ *Dealing with Tough Times*
◎ *Learning to Communicate*
◎ *Understanding Myself*

"Called by Name: A Confirmation Retreat"

As presented, this retreat complements the following Discovering courses:
- *Being Catholic*
- *Gathering to Celebrate*
- *Making Decisions*
- *Seeking Justice*

"Following in the Footsteps of Jesus: A Retreat on Discipleship"

As presented, this retreat complements the following Discovering courses:
- *Becoming Friends*
- *Being Catholic*
- *Meeting Jesus*
- *Seeking Justice*

"By His Cross and Resurrection: A Retreat on Triduum Themes"

As presented, this retreat complements the following Discovering courses:
- *Being Catholic*
- *Celebrating the Eucharist*
- *Exploring the Bible*
- *Meeting Jesus*
- *Praying*
- *Seeking Justice*

"Let's Get Rolling: A Leadership Day for Young Teens"

As presented, this retreat complements the following Discovering courses:
- *Learning to Communicate*
- *Making Decisions*
- *Understanding Myself*

Appendix 2

Connections to the Discovering Program by Discovering Course

Becoming Friends

These HELP retreats complement this course as they are presented:
- ◎ "Let Your Light Shine: An Overnight Retreat on Self-Esteem"
- ◎ "Beneath Our Masks: An Overnight Retreat on Being True to Oneself"
- ◎ "Following in the Footsteps of Jesus: A Retreat on Discipleship"

Being Catholic

These HELP retreats complement this course as they are presented:
- ◎ "Called by Name: A Confirmation Retreat"
- ◎ "Following in the Footsteps of Jesus: A Retreat on Discipleship"
- ◎ "By His Cross and Resurrection: A Retreat on Triduum Themes"

Celebrating the Eucharist

This HELP retreat complements this course as it is presented:
- ◎ "By His Cross and Resurrection: A Retreat on Triduum Themes"

Dealing with Tough Times

This HELP retreat complements this course as it is presented:
- ◎ "Beneath Our Masks: An Overnight Retreat on Being True to Oneself"

Exploring the Bible

This HELP retreat complements this course as it is presented:
- ◎ "By His Cross and Resurrection: A Retreat on Triduum Themes"

Gathering to Celebrate

This HELP retreat complements this course as it is presented:
- ◎ "Called by Name: A Confirmation Retreat"

Learning to Communicate

These HELP retreats complement this course as they are presented:
- ◎ "Beneath Our Masks: An Overnight Retreat on Being True to Oneself"
- ◎ "Let's Get Rolling: A Leadership Day for Young Teens"

Making Decisions

These HELP retreats complement this course as they are presented:
- ◎ "Let Your Light Shine: An Overnight Retreat on Self-Esteem"
- ◎ "Called by Name: A Confirmation Retreat"
- ◎ "Let's Get Rolling: A Leadership Day for Young Teens"

Meeting Jesus

These HELP retreats complement this course as they are presented:
- ◎ "Following in the Footsteps of Jesus: A Retreat on Discipleship"
- ◎ "By His Cross and Resurrection: A Retreat on Triduum Themes"

Praying

This HELP retreat complements this course as it is presented:
- ◎ "By His Cross and Resurrection: A Retreat on Triduum Themes"

Seeking Justice

These HELP retreats complement this course as they are presented:
- ◎ "Called by Name: A Confirmation Retreat"
- ◎ "Following in the Footsteps of Jesus: A Retreat on Discipleship"
- ◎ "By His Cross and Resurrection: A Retreat on Triduum Themes"

Understanding Myself

These HELP retreats complement this course as they are presented:
- ◎ "Let Your Light Shine: An Overnight Retreat on Self-Esteem"
- ◎ "Beneath Our Masks: An Overnight Retreat on Being True to Oneself"
- ◎ "Let's Get Rolling: A Leadership Day for Young Teens"

Acknowledgments (continued)

The retreat "Let Your Light Shine" was originally published in *Growing with Jesus,* by Maryann Hakowski (Notre Dame, IN: Ave Maria Press, 1993). Used with permission of Maryann Hakowski.

The story "Christmas Island" on resource 1 in "Let Your Light Shine" was adapted from a story by Mary Ellen Holmes that appeared in *The War Cry* (Christmas 1989).

Psalm 27 on handout 2 in the retreat "Let Your Light Shine" is adapted from the New Revised Standard Version of the Bible. Copyright © 1989 by the Division of Christian Education of the National Council of the Churches of Christ in the United States of America. All rights reserved.

The activities "Climbing the Walls" on pages 44–45 and "Stand in the Square" on page 45 are adapted from *Building Community in Youth Groups,* by Denny Rydberg (Loveland, CO: Group Books, 1985), pages 36–37 and 48–49. Copyright © 1985 by Thom Schultz Publications.

The activity in part 5 of the retreat "Beneath Our Masks" is adapted from *Do It! Active Learning in Youth Ministry,* revised and updated, by Thom and Joani Schultz (Loveland, CO: Group Publishing, 2000), pages 65–67. Copyright © 2000 by Thom and Joani Schultz.

All other scriptural material is freely paraphrased and is not meant to be used or understood as on official translation of the Bible.

The Nicene Creed, quoted on resource 2 in the retreat "Called by Name," is adapted from *The Rites of the Catholic Church,* volume 1 [New York: Pueblo Publishing Company, 1990], page 204. Copyright © 1976, 1983, 1988, 1990 by Pueblo Publishing Company.